Joseph Wilson Lawrence

Foot Prints

Or Incidents in Early History of New Brunswick

Joseph Wilson Lawrence

Foot Prints
Or Incidents in Early History of New Brunswick

ISBN/EAN: 9783337250829

Printed in Europe, USA, Canada, Australia, Japan

Cover: Foto ©ninafisch / pixelio.de

More available books at **www.hansebooks.com**

Yours Truly
J. W. Lawrence

1783.   1883.
_____

Foot-Prints;

OR,

INCIDENTS IN EARLY HISTORY

OF

NEW BRUNSWICK.

"Its Days should speak, and Multitude of Years Teach Wisdom."

BY

J. W. LAWRENCE,

Corresponding Member New England Historical and Genealogical Society.
Honorary Member Quebec Literary and Historical Society.
Honorary Member Worcester Society of Antiquity.

SAINT JOHN, N. B.:
J. & A. McMILLAN, 98 PRINCE WILLIAM STREET.
1883.

To JOSEPH W. LAWRENCE, ESQ.,

President New Brunswick Historical Society:

SIR,—Feeling that the publication of your paper on "Early Incidents of Saint John History," with suggestions for a series of celebrations in 1883, the Centennial year of the landing of the Loyalists at the mouth of the River Saint John, would give an impetus to your suggestions, we, the undersigned, respectfully request that you will consent to its publication in suitable form.

(Signed) S. JONES, Mayor.

J. C. ALLEN, Chief Justice.

G. E. KING, Judge Supreme Court.

JOHN BOYD, Senator.

ISAAC BURPEE, M. P.

WM. ELDER, M. P. P.

G. M. ARMSTRONG, Rector St. Marks.

D. D. CURRIE, Minister Centenary M. Church.

DAVID S. KERR, Q. C.

LEB. BOTSFORD, Pres't Natural History Society.

WARD CHIPMAN DRURY, Reg'str Deeds & Wills.

A. A. STOCKTON, M.A., LL.B.

St. John, N. B., December, 1881.

Introduction.

A. A. Stockton, M.A., LL.B.

"Incidents in Early History of New Brunswick," it is understood is but the forerunner to other works on kindred topics from the same pen. No more appropriate introduction, therefore, could be prefixed to the following pages than a short biographical sketch of the author.

Joseph W. Lawrence, the President of the New Brunswick Historical Society, was born of Scottish parentage in the City of St. John, N. B., the 28th of February, A. D. 1818. His father was a furniture manufacturer, and for fifty-one years the son followed the same business. The educational advantages of the Province, half a century ago, were small indeed, compared with the present. Notwithstanding these drawbacks, Mr. Lawrence, by dint of close application and study, rose superior to them, and from early boyhood evinced a decided taste for general reading and public debate. He was among the first to organize (in 1835) and to sustain the St. John Young Men's Debating Society, of which he was a prominent member. In 1846 he was married to Miss A. C. Bloomfield, of the city of New York. For over twenty-five years, continuously, he was a Director of the Mechanics' Institute; and as President, in 1849, introduced the late Hon. Joseph Howe, and in 1850, the Hon. Sir Charles Tupper to St. John audiences. The latter, two years ago, addressing a public meeting at the Exhibition building, gracefully referred to the fact. Mr. Lawrence is himself a strong platform speaker, having a clear, ringing voice, and the happy faculty of arresting and holding the attention of his audience.

He has always taken a deep and lively interest in political affairs, and was twice elected to represent his native City in the Legislature of New Brunswick prior to Confederation. In the memorable Session of 1857, he held the floor of the Assembly for over an hour, when His Excellency, Sir J. H. T. Manners-Sutton, came down to dissolve the House.

When the question of Confederating the British North American Provinces into the Dominion of Canada became a vital one in practical politics, he gave it his determined opposition, and continued to do so until the Union was finally consummated. The electorate of New Brunswick, in 1865, pronounced against the proposed Union, and upon the change of Administration in that year, the Chairman of the European and North American Railway Commission (the late Robert Jardine, Esq.) having resigned that position, Mr. Lawrence was appointed to the vacancy. The Administration, led by the Hon. Sir Albert J. Smith, suffered defeat at the polls in 1866, on the question of Confederation, and the new Government insisted upon the displacement of Mr. Lawrence from the Chairmanship of the Railway. His Excellency, Sir A. H. Gordon, for months resisted the demand, but finally yielded, reluctantly, as he was on the eve of leaving the Province, and wished the difficulty removed before the arrival of his successor.

After the accomplishment of Confederation, the route of the Intercolonial Railway became an absorbing question to the people of New Brunswick. A Railway connecting the Confederated Provinces, by the terms of the Imperial Statute, had to be built; but its location was left for future determination. Mr. Lawrence was foremost in the discussion. He published a very able pamphlet, advocating the route by the valley of the St. John. He presented its advantages so clearly, that the Hon. Wm. MacDougall, then Minister of Public Works of Canada, became its firm advocate and supporter.

The next public question of importance to engage Mr. Lawrence's attention, was the Baie Verte Canal. During the Administration of the Hon. Alexander Mackenzie, a Commission, composed of the Hon. Sir Wm. Howland, Toronto; Hon. John Young, Montreal; Peter Jack, Esq., Halifax; and Mr. Lawrence, was appointed to collect information and report upon the practicability of that work. The three gentlemen first named reported adversely to the proposed undertaking; but Mr. Lawrence prepared and published a very valuable and able minority report, which was laid before Parliament.

Of late years he has devoted his time almost exclusively to the collection and arrangement of data concerning the history of this City and Province. No person more suitable could be found for the work. He possesses in an eminent degree the aptitudes of an antiquary; his self-imposed task is, consequently, a labor of love. For many years he has been considered *the* authority on Provincial History, and applications for information from all quarters are numerous. Mr. George Stewart, Jr., in his book on "The Story of the Great Fire in St. John, N. B.," acknowledged his indebtedness. He says: "Before taking leave of my readers, I must publicly thank Mr. Joseph W. Lawrence for his splendid aid which he gave me in furnishing the data and historical information about old churches and other edifices."

In the present work, Mr. Lawrence has made no attempt to weave his many interesting facts into the warp and woof of a completed whole. They would not admit of such treatment. As we, this year, celebrate the completion of our first "Centennial," he has opportunely pointed out some of the "Foot-Prints" which mark the pathway of the Province through the first century of its history.

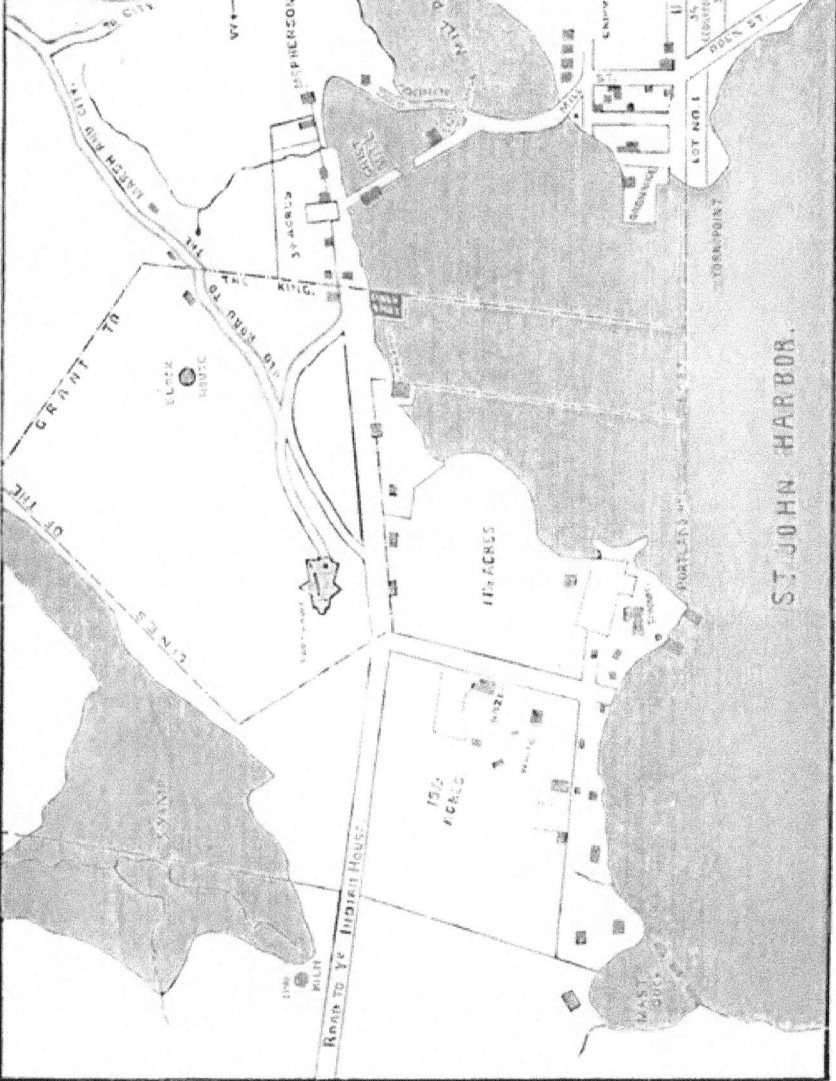

- PLAN OF
- PORTLAND -
- AND PART OF CITY, A.D. 1800 •
- SCALE, 1 inch, 1 furlong •

GERMAIN ST.

PRINCE WILLIAM ST.

STREET

UNION

KING ST.

MARKET SQUARE

ROCK ST

LOT NO 1

YORK POINT

PORTLAND

ST. JOHN HARBOR.

MCPHERSON'S

MILL POND

LINDEN HILL CITY

KINECH RUN LOT

GRANT TO

THE

KING'S

57 ACRES

OLD ROAD TO

BLOCK HOUSE

THE GRANT OF

17 ACRES

152 ACRES

ROAD TO YE INDIAN HOUSE

LOG MILL

Incidents in Early History

OF

NEW BRUNSWICK.

STANDING on the threshold of New Brunswick's first centennial year, it is a fitting time to consider the days of old and the years that are past.

The Loyalists at New York.

At the close of the American Revolution, Sir Guy Carleton, Commander-in-chief at New York, was waited on by the Rev. Samuel Seabury, D. D., and Col. Benjamin Thompson, King's American Dragoons, on behalf of Loyalists desirous of going to Nova Scotia, when it was agreed—

1st. They be provided with proper vessels to carry them, their horses and cattle, as near as possible to the place appointed for the settlers in Nova Scotia.

2nd. That, beside provision for the voyage, one year's provision be also allowed, or money to enable them to purchase.

3rd. That allowance of warm clothing be made, in proportion to the wants of each family.

4th. That an allowance of medicine be granted.

5th. That pairs of mill-stones, necessary iron work for grist mills, and other necessary articles for saw mills, be granted.

(1)

6th. That a quantity of nails, spikes, hoes, axes, spades, shovels, plough irons, and such other farming utensils as shall appear necessary, be provided for them; and also a proportion of window glass.

7th. That tracts of land, free from disputed titles, and conveniently situated, be granted, surveyed and divided at public cost, as shall afford from three hundred to six hundred acres of land to each family.

8th. That over and above, two thousand acres in every Township be allowed for the support of a Clergyman, and one thousand acres for the support of a School, and these lands be unalienable forever.

9th. That a sufficient number of good muskets and cannon be allowed, with proper quantity of powder and ball for their use, to enable them to defend themselves against any hostile invasion.

Agents chosen by the Loyalists.

LIEUT.-COLONEL BENJAMIN THOMPSON.

Lieut.-Col. THOMPSON, Massachusetts Loyalist, at close of the war went to England, received half pay, and was Knighted. At Munich, attained military distinction, and was created Count Rumford. In 1800, returned to England, and founded the Royal Institution of Great Britain. Count Rumford died in France 1814, bequeathing a handsome sum to Harvard College, Massachusetts.

LIEUT.-COLONEL EDWARD WINSLOW.

EDWARD WINSLOW was a Massachusetts Loyalist, and at the evacuation of Boston, 1776, left for New York, when he was appointed Muster Master General of the North American regiments,—a position held to close of war, when he went to Halifax as Secretary to the Commander-in-chief, General Campbell. On the organization of New Brunswick, was one of the twelve Councillors. Col. Winslow settled in York, and was made Surrogate General of the Province; and, although not a member of the Bar, was, on the death of Judge Allen, appointed to his seat on the Bench. In 1808, on the death of Hon. Gabriel G. Ludlow, he succeeded him as President and Commander-in-chief. Judge Winslow died May 13, 1815, aged 69 years.

MAJOR JOSHUA UPHAM.

JOSHUA UPHAM was one of the Members of Council, and one of the first Judges of the Supreme Court. He resided above the French Village, Hammond River, Kings County. While in England, seeking an increase of salary for the Judges, died November 1st, 1808, aged 67 years.

REV. SAMUEL SEABURY, D. D.

Rev. SAMUEL SEABURY returned at close of war to Connecticut, and was chosen by his brother Clergy for the office of Bishop. In 1784 he received consecration in Scotland. On his return to the United States, he stopped at St. John and preached. His daughter Abigail was the wife of Colin Campbell, Clerk of the Supreme Court of New Brunswick. Bishop Seabury died 1796, at the age of 68 years.

REV. JOHN SAYRE.

Rev. JOHN SAYRE, when the war commenced, was Rector of Trinity Church, Fairfield, Connecticut. He drew lot 36 Dock Street. He removed to Maugerville, on the River St. John, and died August 5th, 1784, in his 48th year. His daughter Esther married Christopher Robinson, and shortly after left with him for Upper Canada. Mr. Robinson was appointed Deputy Surveyor General of Crown Lands. He was the father of Sir Beverly Robinson, Chief Justice of Ontario, and grandfather of Hon. John Beverly Robinson, the present Lieutenant Governor of that Province.

AMOS BOTSFORD.

AMOS BOTSFORD, at close of war drew lots in Parr Town. He settled at Sackville. At the first elections, 1785, was returned one of the Members for Westmorland, and at the opening of the Legislature at Parr Town, 1786, chosen Speaker,—position held continuously to death at St. John, March, 1812, then in his 70th year. His son William, afterwards a Judge, the Representative of the County, and three years later was Speaker.

JAMES PETERS.

JAMES PETERS, resident at Gagetown, and for many years one of the Representatives of Queens. He drew lots 11 and 54 Parr Town, the latter in family to this day. The more prominent of his sons were, Hon. Thomas H. Peters, long a resident of Northumberland; the Hon. Charles Jeffrey Peters, twenty years Attorney General; James, a merchant of St. John; William Tyng, a member of the Bar, and Clerk of the Legislative Council; Benjamin Lester, at his death, 1852, at the age of 63 years, Police Magistrate of St. John. The last survivor of the second generation, Hon. Harry Peters, of Gagetown, many years a merchant of St. John, and from 1820 to 1827 one of the Representatives of the City, and three years Speaker; and afterwards Member of the Legislative Council. He died at Gagetown, 1870, aged 82 years.

Arrival of the Loyalists at Parr Town.

In April, 1783, the first fleet left New York for the River St. John[*] with Loyalists. There were about three thousand men, women and children. The landing was the 18th of May, on the present Market Square, from the *Camel*, Capt. Tinker; *Union*, Capt. Wilson; *Aurora*, Capt. Jackson; *Hope*, Capt. Peacock; *Otter*, Capt. Burns; *Spencer*, Capt. ——; *Emmett*, Capt. Reed; *Thames*, Capt. ——; *Spring*, Capt. Cadish; *Bridgewater*, Capt. ——; *Favorite*, Capt. Ellis; *Ann*, Capt. Clark; *Commerce*, Capt. Strong; *William*, Capt. ——; *Lord Townsend*, Capt. Hogg; *Sovereign*, Capt. Stuart: *Sally*, Capt. Bell; *Cyrus*, Capt. ——; *Britain*, Capt. ——; *King George*, Capt. ——. Vessels continued arriving through the summer. In the month of October the fall fleet arrived with twelve hundred. These, with numbers before, found shelter in log houses and bark camps. Transports with troops and stores arrived as late as December. The troops tented through the winter under canvas on the Barrack Square, Lower Cove. Parr Town and Carleton, at the close of 1783, had a population of 5000.

---

[*] The first exploration of the River St. John was made by a party from Massachusetts, 1761, led by Israel Perley. They proceeded to Machias by water, and on through the woods to Oromocto, descending to the River St. John. Of the Maugerville settlement, Mr. Perley was the founder. He died in 1813 in his 74th year. The same year, Fort Frederick (old Fort Latour) was garrisoned by a Highland regiment, and a survey made of the Harbor of St. John by Captain Bruce, of the Royal Engineers. The 28th of August, 1762, James Simonds, James White, Jonathan Leavitt, Francis Peabody, and Hugh Quinton arrived at the mouth of the St. John River from Newburyport. On the evening of the day of arrival, James, son of Hugh Quinton, was born in Fort Frederick, western side of the harbor. Mr. Simonds erected his dwelling on the ruins of an old French fort, Portland Point. At the Upper Cove (Market Slip) Jonathan Leavitt built a schooner as early as 1770, and named her the *Monneguash*, the Indian name of the Peninsula, afterwards Parr Town. Messrs. Simonds, White and Leavitt married daughters of Francis Peabody, who settled at Maugerville on the River St. John. His will was proven and registered the 25th of June, 1773: James Simonds, Judge of Probates; Benjamin Atherton, Registrar.

The garrison at Fort Howe, at this time, was commanded by Major Gilfred Studholm. Parr Town and Carleton was laid out by Paul Bedell,* under his direction. The former, named after Governor Parr, of Nova Scotia; the latter, after Sir Guy Carleton, Commander-in-chief at New York.

The Loyalists received a lot, with five hundred feet of boards, shingles, and bricks. Most of the erections, at first, were log houses; the lumber for roofing. The distribution was under the direction of Major Studholm: 1,664,110 feet of boards, and 1,449,919 shingles were given. After the lines of the streets were run, the trees were cut; the stumps, in many places, were not removed for years. Carting between the Upper and Lower Cove was along the shore: provisions from the beach had to be carried to the dwellings on the back. The only article to hand was firewood, from the lots and streets.

The British Government allowed the Loyalists and their families provisions for the first year; two-thirds for the second; and one-third for the third year.

---

* Paul Bedell drew lot 32, 50 feet on Dock Street, with frontage on the Market Square, to Prince William Street; as his brother Joseph drew lot 33, behind it, with 50 feet on Dock and Prince William, it must in this case have been by selection, and not chance. Paul Bedell died in 1798.

PROVINCE OF NEW BRUNSWICK.

The 16th of August, 1784, the County of Sunbury, Nova Scotia, was established as a Province, with Thomas Carleton, late Colonel 29th regiment, brother of Sir Guy Carleton, as Captain General and Commander-in-chief of New Brunswick, Nova Scotia, and Canada.

In the fall of 1784, Colonel Carleton and family arrived at Halifax from London, after a passage of 56 days. Jonathan Odell, Provincial Secretary, and Ward Chipman, Solicitor General, were passengers. Sunday afternoon, November 21st, they all arrived at Parr Town from Digby in the sloop *Ranger*, Capt. Hatfield, after a passage of six hours. As they passed the Lower Cove, a salute of 17 guns was fired, and on landing at the Upper Cove, the same number from Fort Howe. The Governor and family proceeded to the house of George Leonard, corner of Dock and Union Streets. The day following, His Majesty's commission was read, when Thomas Carleton took the oath required by law, and administered the same to George Duncan Ludlow, James Putnam, Abijah Willard, Gabriel G. Ludlow, Isaac Allen, William Hazen, and Jonathan Odell, they being of the number nominated in the King's instructions to be of His Majesty's Council for New Brunswick. The others named were Beverly Robinson, Sen., Edward Winslow, Daniel Bliss, Joshua Upham, and Gilfred Studholm.*

HEADS OF DEPARTMENTS.

Provincial Secretary, Jonathan Odell.
Surveyor General, George Sproule.
Receiver General, Andrew Rainsford.
Province Treasurer, Richard Seaman.

THE CITY OF SAINT JOHN.

The Charter of St. John was a Royal one, prepared by the acting Attorney General, Ward Chipman. The following refers to the Charter:

---

* Major Gilfred Studholm was in command of Fort Howe at close of the war. He drew two lots on the west side of Prince William Street, adjoining Gilfred, also one adjoining the present City Hall. He also drew a large tract of land at Sussex, Kings County, and removed there. On the division of that Parish, over half a century after, it was named Studholm. His last attendance at Council was at St. John 23rd April, 1787: he was the first of the Councillors who died.

"Sir,—

"The draft of the Charter of the City has been so long delayed, and is of so great length, that I have taken the liberty to send the enclosed without postponing it so long a time as would necessarily take to have a fairer copy made out.

"When the Governor and Council shall have approved of any part of the draft, and filled up the blanks, if they think proper, such sheets may be taken off and be engrossed on parchment, while the remaining parts shall be under consideration.

"I humbly submit whether the City should not be called the City of St. John, instead of the City of St. John's.

"I am, with great respect,
        your most ob't,
              and very humble servant,
                      "WARD CHIPMAN."

"Hon. JONATHAN ODELL, Esq.,
        "Secretary of Council."

The suggestion to call the City (now the oldest in the British Colonies) the City of St. John, in place of St. John's, was adopted, and though nearly a century has gone, and all the actors then on life's stage have passed away, the happy suggestion on the part of Ward Chipman should be named to his praise.

The 18th of May, 1785, the second anniversary of the landing of the first Loyalists, Parr Town and Carleton, with a section of land north of Union Street, the property of Simonds, White, and Hazen, with Navy and Partridge Islands, and the three Islands in the Falls, were incorporated as the City of St. John.

THE FIRST MAYOR OF ST. JOHN.

"*Halifax, January 13th*, 1785.

"My dear Sir,—

"I cannot express how highly and sincerely I am gratified at your first secret respecting Col. Ludlow, of all things possible the most fortunate in my opinion,—a character so dignified, so perfectly unexceptionable, must give dignity to the office.

"The moment the idea of a City was suggested, I cast about to find a man calculated to commence operations as Mayor; there was not, among my many extensive connexions, an individual who was not in some respect or other to my mind exceptionable. Interest, party, ignorance, temper, imperiousness, indolence, were traits that distressed and embarrassed me.

"I dare not think of our friend seriously, for fear that such a circumstance would rather offend than please. The more I considered the business, the more the perplexity increased, and I at last ventured to express my sentiments to the Governor and Mr. Odell.

"I know of no duty that is so irksome and unpleasant as that of giving an opinion of individuals, and yet it is very important.

"The Judge named several persons to me, some of whom I declare I love sincerely, but I was sure that the consequence of either of their appointments to that office would have been unfortunate for themselves, and an injury to the public, and to him I stated my reasons without restraint.

"I have never been an enthusiast for towns and cities, but I declare if this event takes place in all its parts, and Mr. Hardy * is induced to accept the other appointment, I shall expect to see

---

* Elias Hardy was in New York at close of war, practising his profession. In New Brunswick he was known as the London Lawyer. At the election of members for the first House of Assembly, Mr. Hardy was returned for Northumberland, although not residing there. In the second, for St. John. In the celebrated slander trial, 1790, Benedict Arnold vs. Monson Hait, Hardy was Council for Defendant, the Plaintiff retaining Attorney General Bliss and Solicitor General Chipman. In 1790 he was appointed Common Clerk. In the inventory taken after his death, 1799, his library was appraised at Eighteen Pounds. Mr. Hardy married a daughter of Dr. Peter Huggerford, Surgeon in the New York regiment raised by Col. Beverly Robinson. Dr. Huggerford drew a lot in Studholm Street. Like many other leading Loyalists, he early returned. Mr. Hardy, at his death, resided in King Street, third lot south side, east of Germain. Mrs. Hardy, several years afterwards, returned with her family to New York. In 1804 Mrs. Hardy sold one half of lot 417 King Street (Fisher lot, opposite Waverley) to William Melick for £15, and in 1820, the other half to Crookshank & Johnston for £100.

Halifax evacuated by the most respectable of its inhabitants, and Shelburne totally eclipsed, and this immediately. . . . . .
                                        " Your's,
                                                " EDW. WINSLOW.
" WARD CHIPMAN, Esq."

HON. GABRIEL G. LUDLOW,

was a New York Loyalist, and through the war commanded one of the Loyal American regiments. At its close, with other leading Loyalists, he went to England; after remaining there a short time, he came to Parr Town with his brother, Judge Ludlow. He drew three lots in Carleton, a spot formerly used by the French as a garden; for many years it had a fine orchard.

Col. Ludlow was appointed a member of the first Council, and at the incorporation of the City of St. John, Mayor. On the organization, 1787, of the Court of Vice Admiralty, although not a member of the Bar, he was appointed Judge.

In 1795 he resigned the office of Mayor, and in 1803, when Governor Carleton* left for England, Col. Ludlow, as senior Councillor (after Chief Justice), was sworn in at St. John, President and Commander-in-chief, residing at Carleton, except dur-

---

* Thomas Carleton, after a continuous residence in New Brunswick of nineteen years, left with his family for England, intending to return at the end of two years. He remained to his death, retaining the office. In the interim there were eight Administrators, two dying in office. The only announcement of his demise in the New Brunswick press was:

"DIED—At Ramsgate, England, on the 2nd of February, 1817, General Carleton, aged 81 years."

The death of others, hardly less influential, was often as brief. The following shows Governor Carleton, as well as his contemporaries, to have been men of great liberality:

                                        " FREDERICTON, N. B., July, 1798.

"VOLUNTARY CONTRIBUTIONS

in the County of York for carrying on the just and necessary war against all His Majesty's enemies.

" N. B.—The whole of the subscriptions are annual during the war.

ing the meeting of the Legislature. The residence of Col.
Ludlow is standing, and known as the "Old Government
House."

	Army currency.		
	£	s.	d.
His Excellency Lieut.-Gen. Carleton, Lieut.-Governor,	555	11	1
Hon. Chief Justice Ludlow,	55	11	1
Major Robinson's 2nd Batt. Royal Artillery,	95	10	4
King's New Brunswick Regiment,	214	5	8
Rev. George Pidgeon, Rector of Fredericton,	55	11	1
Hon. Jonathan Odell, Provincial Secretary,	33	6	8
George Sproule, Surveyor General,	33	6	8
Lieut. Col. Elligood,	22	4	5
Wm. Hazen, Jr.,	26	15	8
Robert Hazen, Lieut. 60th Regiment, Aid-de-Camp,	26	15	8
David Brown, Assistant Surgeon,	37	10	0
John Murray Bliss, Captain,	5	0	0
Alexander Black, Lieutenant,	25	0	0
William F. Odell, Lieutenant,	5	0	0
Edward Miller, Sergeant,	5	0	0
Peter Frazer,	15	0	0
James Bell,	5	0	0
Andrew Rainsford,	5	0	0
YORK COUNTY MILITIA.			
Hon. Brigadier Isaac Allen,	30	0	0
Col. Richard Armstrong,	15	0	0
Lieut. Col. John Barbarie,	10	0	0
LIGHT INFANTRY.			
Brevet Major Jarvis' company,	47	10	0
Capt. Smith's "	20	10	0
Brevet Major Campbell's "	20	0	0
Capt. Hallett's "	35	7	0
Capt. Griffith's "	30	0	0
Capt. Davidson's "	51	13	0
Capt. Lawrence's "	29	8	0
Capt. Thompson's "	40	0	0
Capt. Willis' "	19	11	6
Capt. Phair's "	16	0	0
Capt. Cooper's "	11	17	6
Joseph Waven, Black Drummer,	2	0	0
Five black men attached to Capt. Davidson's comp'y,	2	15	0

"St. John and other Counties loyally followed in time."

In the graveyard, Carleton, is a stone inside of an iron rail enclosure, with the following inscriptions:

IN

MEMORY

OF THE

HONORABLE GABRIEL G. LUDLOW, ESQ.,

*Late President and Commander-in-Chief
of this Province.*

Born April 16, 1736.

Died February 12, 1808.

SACRED

TO THE MEMORY OF

ANN LUDLOW,

RELICT OF THE LATE GABRIEL G. LUDLOW.

Born Oct. 11, 1743.

Died Dec. 13, 1822.

In Trinity Church, St. John, at the time of its burning, June 20th, 1877, was a tablet to the memory of Col. Ludlow; on it was recorded:

"HE WAS TRULY A GOOD MAN."

Banyer Ludlow, of Westchester, New York, Honorary member of the New Brunswick Historical Society, wrote the President Nov. 15, 1881: "You say I should be present at your Centennial, 1883. If I am alive, and able to travel, I shall be most happy to avail myself of the opportunity of visiting the home and resting place of my great grandfather, Colonel Gabriel G. Ludlow."

THE FIRST COMMON CLERK.

Bartholomew Crannell, the first Common Clerk of St. John, was called Father Crannell, from being the first admitted to the Bar of New Brunswick. In 1744, Mr. Crannell married Miss Van Kleek, of Poughkeepsie; their daughter, Frances, married Thomas Lawton, a merchant of St. John, and Deputy Common Clerk; another married the Rev. John Beardsley, the second Rector of Maugerville. Mr. Crannell died 24th May, 1790, in his 70th year. Among other bequests was Twenty-five Pounds to Trinity Church, St. John.

NEW BRUNSWICK'S FIRST ATTORNEY GENERAL.

"HALIFAX, January 14th, 1875.

"MY DEAR CHIPMAN.

"You will have heard, before this reaches you, that Governor Parr has made me Attorney General here. I am now in the full execution of the office. The warrant has not yet arrived, but I have letters from Sir William P., of the 4th September, acquainting me that Mr. N. was to write me at once.

"Nothing is said respecting my successor in New Brunswick, but as Matthew's warrant for Louisbourg was forwarded by the same opportunity, I think it probable he is not the man. I wish you may be. In the meantime, would it not be well to get an order from your Governor and Council for you to do the duty, and let it be known in England that you are doing it. It will be necessary to have such appointment when grants are to be made, for the King's instructions require the *Attorney General's fiat.* I will furnish you with the form whenever you want it.

"And now my dear Chip., how are you settled? Have you comfortable lodgings, and are you contented? Do you find business enough? How do you like your Province and its prospects? Can I be of service to it or you here?

"Present my compliments to Mr. Odell; let me be remembered to the Chief Justice and his brethren. Write me often, and believe me always truly yours.   The ladies, with me, desire compliments.

"S. S. Blowers.*

"Ward Chipman, Esq."

"Bristol, February, 5th, 1785.

"My Dear Chipman.

"I have just time to acknowledge the receipt of your letters of 6th and 16th of November, from Halifax. Jonathan Bliss, who, I suppose you are apprised, is appointed your Attorney General, is now going to London to prepare for his embarkation for New Brunswick in April next. I intend to send Jonathan out under his care, if in the meantime I receive no letter of discouragement from you. It has been a strange business about your Attorney Generalship. Bliss knew nothing of his appointment till he saw it in the *Court Register*.

"Yours,
"Jonathan Sewell."

Writing Thomas A. Coffin, April 27, 1785, at Halifax, Mr. Sewell says:

"A few days ago I received a letter from our mutual friend Chip. I grieve for the disappointment of his hopes when he received the intelligence of the appointment of Jonathan Bliss as Attorney General."

---

* Samson Salters Blowers graduated in 1763, at Harvard, with Jonathan Bliss. They studied law together in the office of Lieut. Governor Hutchinson. At the evacuation of Boston, 1776, he went to England, and, after a time, to New York, and from there, in 1783, to Halifax. In 1785 he was elected one of the members to the Legislature,—the same year, Jonathan Bliss and Ward Chipman were elected for St. John. In 1799 Attorney General Blowers was appointed Chief Justice of Nova Scotia, with the Presidency of Council. In 1809, Jonathan Bliss attained to the same offices in New Brunswick. In 1833 Chief Justice Blowers resigned office; and in 1842, in his 100th year, died, leaving his wealth to William Blowers Bliss, the second son of the late Chief Justice Bliss of New Brunswick.

ATTORNEY GENERAL BLISS AT HALIFAX.

Edward Winslow, the 29th April, wrote Ward Chipman:

"Two days ago, Jonathan Bliss, young Sewell, Capt. Sproule,* Mrs. Putnam, daughter and son arrived here in thirty days from London. Yesterday I dined with Bliss and Sewell,† who is one of the finest lads I ever saw. I shall pay every possible attention to him. He is extremely anxious to get to New Brunswick. I regret I shall not be able to set off with him. I hope he is to make one of your family."

FROM THE FATHER OF NEW BRUNSWICK'S FIRST LAW STUDENT.

"To all you say about my dear son Jonathan, I have only to answer, that every line drew from me a tear of pleasure. Fond fathers, you know, (or will know soon, for I hear you are in the road to matrimony) are fools. This moment I have received yours of the 7th of July, and have shed another tear of parental joy. Jonathan's and your's, both serve to convince me that he is happy. I long to be with him and you; I am certain I shall be happier when I join you than I have been for ten years past, not to go farther back.

"My wishes, which hitherto have been humble, have now grown ambitious, and terminate in nothing short of a set down at St. John; and, thank God, I can now say that, He willing,

---

* George Sproule, the first Surveyor General of New Brunswick, died at Fredericton 30th November, 1817, aged 76 years, holding the office till his death.

† Jonathan Sewell was born in Boston, 1766. At evacuation, 1776, he left with his parents for England, and was there to after close of war. He was New Brunswick's first law student. After admission to the Bar he practised for a year at St. John, and then removed to Quebec, where he met with great success. In 1793 he was Solicitor General; 1795 Attorney General and Judge of the Court of Vice Admiralty; in 1808, Chief Justice. In 1838 he resigned, receiving from the British Government a pension of £1,000 stg. per annum. He died at Quebec November 12th, 1839, in his 74th year. In the question on the boundary at issue between Ontario and the Dominion Government, the latter largely rely on a decision in 1818 of Chief Justice Sewell.

including the chances of life, health, wind and weather, I shall
positively embark for your New World in April or May next.
My difficulties are removed by a niggardly grant of four hundred
and eighty-six pounds, on a claim for six thousand; however, it
answers my purpose of getting out. I want to spend the remaining days of my pilgrimage in the newest New Jerusalem—the
City of St. John.

"I am pleased you are so hurried in business; it looks well
for you and me also, for I am a derelict here. I have nothing
for it but your Bar.*

"Yours,
"Jonathan Sewell.

"Ward Chipman, Esq."

Jonathan Sewell, a graduate of Harvard in 1767, was Attorney General of Massachusetts Bay. Having resigned that
office before the war, was appointed Judge of the Court of Vice
Admiralty. At the evacuation of Boston, 1776, he went to
England with his wife and two boys, remaining there to his
leaving for New Brunswick. Mrs. Sewell was a sister of the
wife of John Hancock, the first signer of Independence. Mr.
Sewell died at St. John, 1796, at the age of 68 years.

THE WARDS OF ST. JOHN.

The City of St. John, at its incorporation, had four Wards
on the East side, and two on the Carleton side of the harbor, the

---

*"The upper and the lower mill
    Fell out about their water;
To war they went—that is to law,
    Resolved to give no quarter.

"A lawyer was by each engaged,
    And hotly they contended;
When fees grew slack, the war they waged,
    They judged were better ended.

"The heavy costs remained still,
    Were settled without pother,
One lawyer took the upper mill,
    The lower mill the other."

former occupying angles with the dividing streets, Duke and Sydney. Several of the streets east of Sydney had names at first different from the streets west. The prolongation of Duke was Morris; Princess, St. George; St. James, Stormont; King, Great George street.

Consequent on the depopulation of Duke and Sydney Wards, fronting on the back shore, the Ward divisions in 1803 were changed, giving each a frontage on the harbor, with King, Duke and St. James streets the dividing lines.

NAMES OF THE WARDS.

The Wards on the East side were, King, Queen, Duke and Sydney. Why not have chosen Prince, in place of the latter? as better harmonizing with the other names.

SECRETARY OF STATE FOR THE COLONIES.

As the appointment to the Provincial offices were in the gift of the Colonial Secretary, who held the office at this time the following tells:

" *To our trusty and well beloved* WARD CHIPMAN, Esq.

"We have thought fit hereby to authorize and require you forthwith to cause Letters Patent, under the Seal of our Province of New Brunswick in America, constituting and appointing him, the said Ward Chipman, our Solicitor General of and in our said Province; to have, hold, exercise and enjoy the said office of our Solicitor General unto him the said Ward Chipman during our pleasure, and his residence within our said Province, together with all and singular the rights, salaries, allowances, fees, profits, privileges and emoluments thereunto belonging or appertaining; and for so doing this shall be your warrant, and so we bid you farewell.

"Given at our Court of St. James, the nineteenth day of August, 1784, in the 24th year of our reign.

"By His Majesty's command,

"SYDNEY."

B

The Wards on the West side were, Guy and Brook, named after Guy Carleton, Commander-in-Chief at New York, and Brook Watson, head of the Commissariat department. At the evacuation of New York, 25th November, 1783, Brook Watson left for London, and early attained distinction. In 1786 the British Government secured him, for three lives, a pension of £500 stg. per annum.

Jonathan Sewell, Sen., wrote Ward Chipman from Bristol, 1785:

"Brook Watson, who is an Alderman for London and a member of Parliament, and still rising to greater importance, had asked two favors,—one for G. Brindley, and the other I forget who. I cannot think their interests could have been injured by Mr. Watson speaking a word for me and another for you. I had no kind of claim on Mr. Watson, beyond the merit of my cause, and therefore have no cause for complaint,— only for lamentation."

Gregory Townsend, of the Commissariat department, wrote Ward Chipman, April, 1785:

"With respect to the appointment of Attorney General, your doubts and fears are at an end long ere this. As to the Advocate Generalship, I wish you had it with all my heart; but how I can be instrumental in procuring it for you, I do not at present foresee. Mr. Watson, you know, is the only person to whom I can have any recourse on such an occasion; but such have been the delays and impediments thrown in the way of his applications in behalf of the Commissariat folks, that he will not ask anything more at present."

PROVINCE AGENT,— LONDON.

At the meeting of the Legislature, 1786, Brook Watson was appointed Agent for the Province at London, a position held to 1794. At the Session of that year, the following was

"*Resolved*, This House, taking into consideration the necessity of having an Agent residing in England, and His Majesty's service having required the attendance of *Brook Watson*, Esquire, late member of Parliament and Agent of this Province, with His MAJESTY's forces on the Continent;

"*Resolved*, That the thanks of this House be communicated to *Brook Watson*, Esquire, late Agent of this Province, for his past services."

Brook Watson was extensively engaged in commercial pursuits with William Goodall and John Turner, under the firm of Brook Watson & Co. They had extensive relations for years with New Brunswick. In 1801, a St. John merchant failed, owing the house £5,522 sterling.

Before the war, Brook Watson was a merchant of Boston, and in 1763, with others, obtained from the Nova Scotia Government the grant of the Township of Cumberland, Nova Scotia.

Through the war, Brook Watson was known as the Wooden legged Commissary. In 1774, he was a passenger from Boston for England. Among others was Copley, the celebrated portrait painter. To him he related the following :

"When a youth he was bathing in the harbor of Havana, and the leg was taken off by a shark; it returned for another attack just as he was rescued by a boat from the shore."

In 1778, Copley painted a picture of the scene, representing Watson at the moment of his rescue.

Watson enjoyed relating the following:

"At an inn, the servant, in taking off his boots, was warned that if he pulled too hard he would bring the leg with it. To the inexpressible horror of the man, he found leg as well as boot in his hands. Recovering from the shock, and finding the leg could be replaced, 'he begged to know how the gentleman had lost it?' Watson promised to tell him, on one condition,—that he would not ask a second question. Assenting, 'Boots' heard it was bit off; at which, rubbing and scratching his head, he exclaimed, 'How I wish I could ask one more.'"

But for his timely rescue, there would have been no Watson Street, and no Brook's Ward in Carleton, for there would have been no Brook Watson in 1783 with the ear of the Government.

STREETS OF ST. JOHN.

The northern boundary of Parr Town was Union Street, first named Gilfred. All north to the Kennebeccasis was claimed by Simonds, Hazen, and White, under the grant of 1765 from the Nova Scotia Government. At the Incorporation of the City of St. John, 1785, the land to the present City Road was included in the Charter, with the ownership as before. The names of the streets north of Union differ from those south. The continuation of Dock Street is Mill; Germain, Wellington Row; Charlotte, Coburg; Sydney, Waterloo.* To 1816, the latter was called the Old Westmorland Road. After this, Brussels Street was laid out. All the land from † Waterloo Street to Courtenay Bay, north of Union, belonged to James Simonds. The events of the early years of the century on the Continent of Europe left their impress for all time in the names of Wellington, Waterloo† and Brussels Streets.

DOCK STREET.

Of the Parr Town streets, Dock was the only one not at right angles, as it had to follow the shore. Lot number one, at its north-west corner, extending to the water, was drawn by Thomas Leonard. On it was "York Point," the northern bound of the

---

* A public meeting was held at the City Hall, Market Square, 11th December, 1815, in behalf of families of killed and wounded in the Battle of Waterloo. The Hon. Ward Chipman in the chair. Committees were appointed, and £1,472 15s. 6d. collected. The subscribers of £20 and upwards were: William Pagan, £50; Hugh Johnston, Sen., £50; Henry Gilbert, £50; Ward Chipman, £30; William Hazen, £30; Ezekiel Barlow, £30; John Robinson, £30; William Black, £30; John Coffin, £30; Thomas Millidge, £25; James Codner, £20; William Donald, £20; Robert Parker, Sen., £20; Ward Chipman, Jun., £20; John Ward, £20; John M. Wilmot, £20; Munson Jarvis, £20. A subscription like this in St. John before the close of its first third of a century, is an honorable record. The first of the subscribers who died was William Hazen, Sheriff of St. John and Province Treasurer, February 14th, 1816, aged 48 years. The last, Henry Gilbert, at the age of 84 years, July 11th, 1869.

† The stairs at the end of the South Wharf—the Ferry landing to 1838—was named Waterloo; the North Wharf stairs, Trafalgar. The street opened west of Dock, early in the century, was named Nelson in 1817. The four City Engines were, the Wellington, Waterloo, Nelson and Smyth.

Upper Cove. On the "Point" the "Victoria" Warehouse stands, erected since the fire of 1877. Lot number thirty-nine was opposite number one, extending halfway up Union to Prince William Street. It was drawn by George Leonard;* the adjoining one, thirty-eight, was drawn by his son.† On the two lots a fine residence was built, and the grounds tastefully laid out. The house stood back from Dock Street, with a lawn and terrace in front. For many years it was the fashionable section of St. John. On the arrival of Governor Carleton, 1784, the Leonard House was prepared for him. At the death of General Smyth, 1823, it was his city residence.

First Marriage at Parr Town.

On a tombstone, Sussex, King's County, is the following:

IN MEMORY OF

LIEUT. ANDREW STOCKTON,

Born at PRINCETON, NEW JERSEY, *January 3rd,* 1760, *and Died at* SUSSEX VALE, *May 8th,* 1821.

ALSO, HANNAH, HIS WIFE,

Born in the STATE OF NEW YORK, *and Died in* KINGS COUNTY, *October* 1, 1793,

Aged 25 *years and* 4 *months.*

LIEUT. STOCKTON ‡

was married in the City of Saint John, then called

PARR TOWN,

The 4th April, 1784, *by*

The HON. GEORGE LEONARD,

which was the first Marriage in the Town.

---

*Hon. George Leonard was born at Plymouth, New England, 28th November, 1742. After a short residence at St. John, he removed to Sussex, King's County, where he had a large tract of valuable land. For many years he was a member of the Council. Mr. Leonard died the 1st of April, 1826.

† George Leonard, Jun., his son, was an Attorney-at-Law at St. John. He removed to Sussex, and was drowned in the Creek, falling from a log while crossing, 14th October, 1818.

‡ Lieut. Andrew Stockton has living in New Brunswick 14 grand-children, 43 great grand-children, and 54 great great grand-children; besides descendants living in Ontario, Australia, and the United States.

KING STREET.

King Street, one of the chief thoroughfares of St. John, has a breadth of a hundred feet. To this, the preservation of the northern portion of the city was due the afternoon of the great fire, June 20th, 1877.

The old two story building at the corner of the Market Square and King Street, was erected shortly after the landing of the Loyalists by Charles McPherson,* and known as the Coffee House. For nearly half a century it was the centre of fashionable gatherings, festivities and meetings, political, social, and moral. The name best known in connection with it was "Cody."† The Coffee House,‡ for nearly seventy years, passed through perils

---

* Charles McPherson was a Highlander. When the war commenced, he arrived at New York with a Scotch regiment: at the peace came to Parr Town.

MARRIED, September 19th, 1811, by the Rev. Dr. Byles, Rector, Daniel Leavitt to Catherine, daughter of Charles McPherson.

MARRIED, April 16th, 1814, by the Rev. Roger Veits, Assistant Minister, Capt. Francis Leavitt to Mary, daughter of Charles McPherson.

MARRIED, November 5, 1814, by the Rev. George Pidgeon, Rector, John Fairclough, merchant, to Annabella, daughter of Charles McPherson.

Mr. Fairclough died on passage from West Indies, 1818.

MARRIED, May 31st, 1820, by the Rev. Robert Willis, Rector, Capt. Ambrose Perkins to Mrs. Amelia Fairclough, daughter of Charles McPherson.

Mr. McPherson died at his residence, corner of King and Cross Streets, July 26th, 1823, aged 70 years.

† William G. Cody purchased the Coffee House and commenced business May 18th, 1803, continuing for over twenty years. Having the contract for the erection of the Soldiers' Barracks, Lower Cove, he sustained a great loss consequent on its being blown down the night of 31st December, 1819, in the storm in which the brig *Mary*, Capt. Bell, was lost on Partridge Island. Mr. Cody removed in 1824 to Loch Lomond, and erected the house known of late years as the "Ben Lomond House." The following is one of the family incidents of the year the "Old Coffee House" was opened : Married, October 21st, 1803, by the Rev. Dr. Byles, Rector of St. John, Mr. Richard Whiteside to Jane, daughter of William G. Cody. Mr. Cody died at Loch Lomond, August 25th, 1840, aged 70 years.

‡ *Editorial, 24th October*, 1786.—" Those gentlemen who wish and intend to encourage the Rev. Mr. Frazer to settle in this City, are requested to meet at the Coffee House, to-morrow evening at 7 o'clock. It is expected every person thus inclined will not fail to attend, that it may be known, with certainty, what salary will be promised Mr. Frazer."

A VIEW OF KING STREET.

by fire. In 1853 it was taken down, and the Imperial Buildings erected by the late John Gillis, Esq.

THE OLD KIRK.

It was not until 1814 anything was done. That year the two Germain Street lots were bought for £250, granted by the House of Assembly. Building Committee: William Pagan, Hugh Johnston, Sen., John Thomson, James Gregor, John Currie, William Donaldson, and Alexander Edmunds; Laughlan Donaldson, Secretary. The first settled Minister of the Church of Scotland was the Rev. George Burns, D. D., who arrived at St. John Sunday morning, 25th May, 1817, and in the evening preached in the "Kirk,"—of late years known as St. Andrew's Church, from the text, "I was glad when they said unto me let us go into the house of the Lord." In the fire of 1877 the first and oldest Presbyterian Church in New Brunswick was swept away.

Dr. Burns, in 1831, returned to Scotland. He died in Edinburgh, February 5th, 1876, in his 86th year.

The opposite side of King Street, facing the Market Square, for two-thirds of a century, has been known as "Barlow's Corner." In 1789 the lot with the erections was bought by Judge Putnam for £350. In 1814, his son James sold the same to Ezekiel Barlow for £2,000 in Mexican dollars,—the purchaser wheeling the money in two loads to the office of Ward Chipman. "*Labor omnia vincit.*" The old buildings were removed, and the one seen in the view of King Street completed in 1816 for a residence, with office and stores for its owner. In the spring of 1838 Mr. Barlow died, at the age of 79 years. He was associated in commerce with his sons Thomas and Ezekiel.

On the lot where the Royal Hotel stands was the Mallard House. In it the first Parliament of New Brunswick was opened February, 1786.

HISTORIC BUILDING.

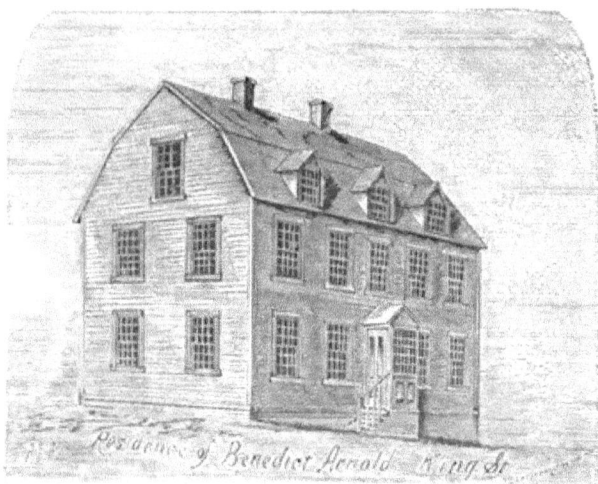

Residence of Benedict Arnold King St

John Porteous drew lot 406, corner of King and Cross Streets, and erected the building in which from 1787 to 1791, General Benedict Arnold lived. After Arnold's return to England it was purchased of the agent of Mr. Porteous by Attorney General Bliss for £350. In the deed it is stated as lately occupied by Benedict Arnold. It was the residence of Mr. Bliss * until his

---

* In 1790, Attorney General Bliss married a daughter of the Hon. John Worthington, of Springfield, Mass.; she died at the King Street residence April 19th, 1799, in her fortieth year, leaving four sons, all born in the old historic dwelling. Their eldest son, John Worthington Bliss, died there Jan. 6th, 1810, aged 19 years, and, with his mother, was buried in the "Old Grave Yard." Lewis, the second son, died in London September 7th, 1882, in his 89th year: In early life he was in the counting house of John Black & Co., St. John. William Blowers, the third son, resided in Halifax, and at his death, March 16th, 1874, in his 79th year, was a Judge of the Supreme Court. Hon. W. H. Odell, Bishop Binney of Nova Scotia, and Bishop Kelly, formerly of Newfoundland, married daughters. Two sons are Clergymen, and reside in England. Henry Bliss, the youngest of the sons of the late Chief Justice, was a member of the Bar, and for half a century resided in London; and for many years agent for New Brunswick: He died July 31st, 1873, in his 76th year. The Chief Justice died at Fredericton October 1st, 1822, aged 80 years. Although in no family burial plot, where side by side they rest, their names live in New Brunswick history on the costly Memorial Window in Trinity Church, St. John, placed there by the last of the second generation, Lewis Bliss.

removal to Fredericton, after his appointment of Chief Justice. In 1811, it was purchased by Charles McPherson. In later years it was converted into stores and offices, and known as the Bragg Building. Like the old Coffee House, for over seventy years it escaped the peril of fire, and was taken down to give place to brick stores.

Another of the historic spots was the corner of King and Charlotte Streets: there, the 28th day of September, 1816, the corner stone of the Masonic Hall was laid with Masonic honors by Thomas Wetmore, Grand Master. It early passed into the hands of Israel Lawson, the Masons meeting there until its sale to the St. John Hotel Company, 1836.

The hotel was opened by Cyrus Stockwell, of Boston, November 27th, 1837. In its long room, concerts, lectures and balls were given for many years, superseding the old Coffee House.

Town Lot Ticket.

This may certify that Thatcher Sears is the rightful owner of Lot No. 397 in Parr Town, being forty feet by one hundred,—having complied with the terms of receiving it.

By order of the Directors * of the Town
at the entrance of the River,
OLIVER ARNOLD.

In the view of King Street, the flag shows the residence of Thatcher Sears.

---

* The Directors were: Rev. John Sayre, George Leonard, William Tyng, James Peters, and Gilfred Studholm. The Secretary, Oliver Arnold, shortly after settled at Sussex Vale. In 1792 he was ordained by Bishop Inglis of Nova Scotia, and appointed Rector of Sussex, holding it until his death in 1834, at the age of 79 years.

William Tyng in the war was a Commissary. In the laying out of Parr Town he received ten lots, north side of Princess Street (first called Tyng Street), from Prince William to Germain Street. He was the second Sheriff of Queens. He early returned to the United States, and died at Gorham, near Portland, December 10th, 1807, aged 70 years.

PUBLIC DRINKING FOUNTAIN.

The first child born at Parr Town was a daughter of Thatcher Sears, at the time living in a tent on the Market Square. *

The following refers to the young lady :

HYMENEAL.—Married, at Trinity Church, Monday, February 10, 1823, by the Rev. Robert Willis, Rector, Samuel Bagshaw, Esq., merchant, to Nancy, second daughter of the late Thatcher Sears, Esq.

PRINCE WILLIAM STREET.

In early years, Prince William was the fashionable street for residences, and later, for business, merchants residing over their stores. The oldest building in St. John is the Crookshank house, in that street, erected by John Colville, one of the first merchants. He died there, November 7th, 1808, aged 70 years. His wife was a daughter of Capt. George Crookshank, a Scotchman, who sailed out of New York through the war. The late Robert W. and Andrew Crookshank were sons. He died at St. John, 1797.

Of the officials who resided in Prince William Street, and died in the last century, was Abraham DePeyster, Province Treasurer.

From the first, to the great fire of 1877, Prince William Street was the head-quarters of the Newspaper Press. At No. 59, Lewis & Ryan issued the first newspaper at Parr Town :

---

* PUBLIC DRINKING FOUNTAIN.

WILLIAM MACARA SEARS, son of John, and grandson of Thatcher Sears, was brought up to the drug business, succeeding John M. Walker on his retirement. Other engagements requiring his attention, he early left it. On the death of Mr. Walker, he was one of his Executors. The 18th May, 1882, Mr. Sears became a Life Member of the Historical Society. At the celebration of the 99th anniversary of the landing of the Loyalists, held at the Mechanics' Institute in the evening, he was present. The last act of his life was the presentation to the City of the Drinking Fountain on the Market Square, where the first landing of the Loyalists was made. The Cartmen, as a mark of appreciation, had an Address and Testimonial to present him on the afternoon of the 23rd September, but, being ill, he was unable to receive it. The day following he died, at the age of 32 years.

Vol. I.   *THE ROYAL*   No. 1.

S^T. JOHN'S GAZETTE,

AND NOVA-SCOTIA INTELLIGENCER:

THURSDAY, DECEMBER 17, 1783.

SHEFFIELD STREET.

The original name of Sheffield was South Street, a name suggestive from being the southern of the Parr Town streets.

The land south of Sheffield Street was outside of the bounds of Parr Town, and reserved by the Government. From 1820 to the removal of the troops, it was occupied by them.

After whom was Sheffield Street named? In 1781, John Baker Holroyd was raised to the Irish Peerage, as Baron Sheffield of Dunamore; in 1802, was made a Baron of the United Kingdom; and in 1806 advanced in the Irish Peerage to the Earldom of Sheffield.

EARL SHEFFIELD A CITIZEN OF ST. JOHN.

At a Court of the Mayor, Aldermen and Assistants of the City of St. John, in Common Council assembled, at the City Hall* of the said City, Friday, the 15th March, 1805, Present:

---

* From 1797, for nearly one third of a century, the building on the Market Square was called the City Hall; the basement at first was a general store; the first flat, with entrance from King Street, was occupied as the City market; the upper story, with a platform the length of the building, was used for the Courts and the Council Chamber, to their removal to new Court House, King Square, 1830. In 1837 it was taken down to give place to the brick building burnt in the fire of 1841. In this the Civic offices were in the second story; the lower portions being occupied by butchers and as a Country market, with a section of the basement as a Lock-up.

The last trial for a capital offence in the old Court House was at the January Term, 1828, Hon. Judge Chipman presiding:

Patrick Burgen, a boy of 18 years, was placed at the Bar, charged with entering the dwelling, in the *night*, of his master, John B. Smith, manufacturer of ginger beer, corner of Union Street and Drury Lane, and robbing the

OLD CITY HALL.

C

His Worship the Mayor, WILLIAM CAMPBELL.

Aldermen: GILBERT,   *Assistants:* MILES,
JOHNSTON,   WETMORE,
GARRISON,   HARDING,
WHITNEY.   KETCHUM,
                        LINGTHWAITE.

Resolved, That the thanks of this Corporation be given to the Right Honorable Lord Sheffield for his Lordship's exertions, by his late as well as former publications, in support of the British Navigation Laws, on which the prosperity of the Empire at large, and more particularly of this and His Majesty's other North American Provinces, so greatly depends.

Resolved, That the Freedom of the City be humbly presented to His Lordship, in a box to be made of the wood of this country,

---

till of one quarter of a dollar. He was arrested the day after, by John McArthur, constable.

The prosecuting officer, Clerk of the Crown, John Thomas Murray, Esq. The Court assigned William B. Kinnear Counsel for the prisoner, as to questions of law, not being allowed then to refer to questions of fact, or address the Jury.

PETIT JURY.

John Cunningham, *Foreman.*	Gilbert T. Ray,	Isaac Flewelling,
William Cormick,	M. J. Lowrey,	Nehemiah Vail,
Amos Robertson,	Wm. Stout,	George Hutchinson,
David Schurman,	James Rankin,	William B. Cox.

As the evidence of guilt was clear, no other course was open to the Jury than a verdict of Guilty,—with this was a recommendation to *mercy.* Yet, the Judge, in sentencing the prisoner to be *executed,* told him there was no hope for mercy, and he should lose no time in preparing for death.

A petition was sent to the Lieut. Governor, Sir Howard Douglas, asking the interposition of the Prerogative in behalf of the prisoner. Yet, notwithstanding the recommendation of the Jury, and the Coronation oath of the Sovereign, requiring "His Majesty to cause *Law* and *Justice* in *Mercy* to be executed in all his judgments," the law was allowed to take its course, and Patrick Burgen, the 21st of February, 1828, was executed from the second story window of the "Old Gaol." The executioner was Blizard Baine, an Englishman, undergoing sentence of two years for robbery. In addition to release from prison, he received from Sheriff White Ten Pounds. Baine lost no time in leaving the city.—*From Manuscript: The Early Lawyers and Old Judges of New Brunswick, and their Times.*

and that a picture from an engraved likeness of His Lordship, presented to this Board by the Honorable George Leonard, Esq., be enclosed in a suitable frame and hung up in the City Hall, in grateful remembrance of his public services.

Resolved, That the Recorder of this City be requested to transmit the foregoing Resolutions in such manner as may be most respectful, requesting His Lordship's acceptance of the gratitude of this Court.

A PORTRAIT OF EARL SHEFFIELD.

In 1806, a full size portrait of His Lordship was received from England, and placed behind the Speaker's Chair, where it remained to the summer of 1820, in which year a Coat of Arms was purchased for the House of Assembly by the Province Agent in London. On its arrival, by order of Governor Smyth, it took the place of Earl Sheffield, who was removed to Government House.

THE HOUSE vs. HIS EXCELLENCY.

House of Assembly, Wednesday, January 31st, 1821.

Mr. *Ward Chipman* moved the following order:

Ordered, That the Portrait of Lord Sheffield, which has been removed from its former place over the *Speaker's* Chair, be forthwith restored to the same.

On the question, the House divided, *Yeas,* 12; *Nays,* 11.

Saturday, 3rd February, 1821.

On motion of Mr. *Chipman,*

Resolved, That the Portrait of Lord Sheffield, instead of being restored to its former place over the *Speaker's* Chair, as directed in the resolution of Wednesday last, be placed in such other part of the House as the *Speaker* may direct.

On the return of the portrait to the Province Hall, it was placed by the Speaker, William Botsford, in the Speaker's room, leaving the Royal Arms behind the Chair.

EARL SHEFFIELD.

Shortly after the arrival of Sir Wm. Colebrook to assume the Governorship, 1841, His Lordship, at the request of Sir William, was sent to Government House, where the picture was nearly ruined by his boy's having made a target of it for shooting arrows at. After Sir William left the Province, the Hon. R. L. Hazen, on learning its state, had it sent to Boston and repaired. On its return, it found a place until the night of the fire, 1880, in the Legislative Council Chamber in the Province Hall.*

Earl Sheffield was three times married; the last Countess was Lady North, daughter of the second Earl of Guilford. His Lordship died in 1831, aged 86 years, at his seat, Sheffield Park, Sussex, leaving one son and one daughter.

CITY FESTIVITIES.

On the evening of the 24th October, 1821, Lieut. Governor Smyth gave a Ball in the Madras School Room, King's Square, St. John, in honor of the Coronation of George IV. Upwards of 200 ladies and gentlemen were present.

The day following, being the 38th anniversary of the landing of the Loyalists from the fall fleet, it was deemed an era justly consecrated to Loyalty and Patriotism. That all ranks might participate in the joy, three tables were spread on King

---

* OTHER PORTRAITS.

Message from His Excellency the Lieutenant Governor:

"FREDERICTON, 11th February, 1822.

"The Lieut. Governor is much gratified to have it in his power to present to the House of Assembly full length portraits of their late Majesties — King George the Third and Queen Charlotte — feeling assured, from the loyal principles which instigated the vote of the last Session for providing the King's picture, that such portraits will be acceptable to the House."

THE ROYAL ARMS.

In the Journals, 1821, is the following: "To Thomas Bonner, Esq., the Provincial Agent, London, the sum of Thirty Pounds, sterling, being the balance due him of the amount for procuring the ROYAL ARMS."

The fine, full length oil painting over the Speaker's Chair in the "Old Province Hall," was the portrait of Lord Glenelg, Colonial Secretary, 1837.

Square, and at one o'clock, an Ox, roasted whole, was conveyed to each, amid the shouts and acclamations of the people.

In the evening, a grand dinner was given in the School Room, Governor Smyth* being present, with Col. Drury† in the Chair. Salutes were fired, rockets sent up, and the band of the 74th regiment played. His Excellency ordered roast beef and plum pudding for the prisoners in gaol.

The Fiftieth Anniversary of the Landing of the Loyalists.

The 18th May, 1833, was ushered in at St. John by the firing of cannon. In the evening a dinner was given by the Corporation in the Masonic Hall, head of King Street. The chair was taken by the Mayor of the City, John M. Wilmot, Esq. On his right was the Lieut.-Governor, Sir Archibald Campbell; on his left the Father of the City, the venerable John Ward, Esq.

The speakers were: Judge Bliss, Judge Chipman, Attorney General Peters, Solicitor General Parker, Col. Turner, Inspecting Field Officer, Major Graves, Hon. John Simcoe Saunders, Stephen Humbert, Aldermen Harding and Van Horne. When the toast, "The day we celebrate," was given, a salute of fifty guns was fired by the City Artillery from King Square.

To the toast, "The Chief Justice, their Honors the Judges of the Supreme Court and the Professional gentlemen of the Bar; may they ever maintain and support the principles of Justice and Honor," Solicitor General Robert Parker replied.

THE TOAST OF THE DAY.

"The land our ancestors left, and the land we live in; both inhabited from one common parent, and enjoying, though under

---

* Major General George S. Smyth, the second Lieut.-Governor, died at Fredericton during the sitting of the Legislature, after an illness of ten days, aged 56 years, March 27, 1823.

† Col. Charles Drury, in his early days, was an officer in the British Army. Marrying a daughter of Hon. William Hazen, led to his settling in New Brunswick. For many years he held the office of Postmaster at St. John and Registrar of Deeds and Wills. Col. Drury died at his residence, Newlands, two miles from the city, October 24th, 1836, at the age of 53 years.

OLD GERMAIN STREET METHODIST CHURCH.

different governments, the blessings of freedom ; may old animosities be forgotten, and the present good understanding continued."

His Worship the Mayor provided roast beef and plum pudding for the prisoners in gaol.

THE CENTENNIAL OF METHODISM.

The 100th anniversary of the founding of the Methodist Church, by John Wesley, was celebrated the 17th August, 1839, in the old Germain Street Methodist Church,* St. John, when a subscription of five thousand eight hundred dollars was made. The day following, the Centenary Church, St. John, was opened for service.

THE SACKVILLE ACADEMY.

The Mount Allison Academy, Sackville, took form that year. The following tells the history of its birth, in "thoughts that breathe and words that burn" :—

ST. JOHN, N. B., *January 4th*, 1839.

REV. AND DEAR SIR:—My mind of late has been much impressed with the importance of that admonition of the wise man, "Train up a child in the way he should go, and when he is old he will not depart from it."

The establishment of schools in which pure religion is not only taught but constantly brought before the youthful mind, and represented to it as the basis and groundwork of all happiness which man is capable of enjoying here on earth, and eminently calculated to form the most perfect character, is, I think, one of the most efficient means, in the order of Divine Providence, to bring about the happy result spoken of by the wise man.

It is, therefore, under this impression, connected with a persuasion of my accountability to that gracious being, whom I would ever recognize as the source of all the good that is done in the earth, that I now propose through you to the British Conference, and to the Wesleyan missionaries in the Provinces of New Brunswick and Nova Scotia, to purchase an eligible site and erect suitable buildings in Sackville, in the county of Westmorland, for the establishment of a school of the description mentioned, in which, not only the

---

* The 24th September, 1791, John Abraham Bishop arrived at St. John from England, and shortly after organized a Methodist Society, at the house of Mr. Kelly, corner of Princess and Charlotte Streets. Christmas Day, 1791, service was held in the building until that time used by the Church of England. On Christmas Day, 1808, the Rev. William Bennett opened the Germain Street Church, which was swept away in the fire of 1877.

elementary but the higher branches of education may be taught, and to be altogether under the management and control of the British Conference in connexion with the Wesleyan Missionaries in these Provinces.

If my proposal should be approved of, and the offer I now make accepted, I will proceed at once to make preparation, so that the buildings may be erected in the course of next year; and I will, as a further inducement, by the blessing of God, give towards the support of the school, one hundred pounds per annum for ten years. I shall be glad to hear that my offer is accepted; and to have the earliest information of your decision on the subject, and am,

Rev. and dear Sir,

Yours sincerely,

C. F. ALLISON.

REV. W. TEMPLE.

At a meeting at St. John, May, 1839, the historic year of Methodism, the offer was accepted, and a committee appointed to act with the donor.

On the 9th of July, 1840, the corner stone was laid by Mr. Allison.

"The foundation stone of this building, I now proceed to lay, in the name of the Holy Trinity, Father, Son and Holy Ghost; and may the education ever to be furnished by the Institution be conducted on Wesleyan principles, to the glory of God and the extension of His cause.—AMEN."

Monument in Sackville graveyard:

In memory of

CHARLES F. ALLISON, ESQ.

He fell asleep in Jesus,

November 20, A. D. 1858, aged 63 years.

"Blessed are the dead who die in the Lord from henceforth; yea, saith the Spirit, that they may rest from their labors, and their works do follow them."

"In all the relations of life he eminently adorned the doctrine of God his Saviour by a blameless and beneficent character, which reflected with peculiar lustre the meekness and gentleness of Christ, firmly attached to the principles and connexion of Methodism. He was also a lover of all good men, and rejoiced in the spread of the religion of Christ by whatever agency achieved, having lived to see the noble institution founded by his munificence occupying a high position, and exercising a wide and salutary influence."

In 1851 the Government of New Brunswick appointed Mr. Allison to a seat in the Legislative Council,* a position he declined.

---

*The last act of Governor Smyth was the offer of a seat in the Council to the late Thomas Millidge, Esq., of St. John. It was declined. Mr. Millidge died 21st August, 1838, aged 62 years.

CHARLES F. ALLISON, ESQ.

New Brunswick's Centennial Year.

In the City founded by the Loyalists, and where they landed in 1783, a Hall for a Public Library, Reading Room, Museum, and Art Gallery, and for the preservation of historic papers and relics, would be a fitting memorial, the windows to illustrate the progress of the century in Arts, Science, Commerce and Manufactures. While a memorial to the founders of New Brunswick, and to the century, the work within would be eminently intellectual, social and moral.*

On the Government of the Province it has unquestionable claims, for while local in its habitation, its work will permeate every corner of New Brunswick. The corner stone should be laid the 18th May, 1883, and as the centennial of the City of St. John (the oldest in the British Colonies) will be the 18th May, 1885, the Hall should be completed by that time in all its appointments. "Every one helping his neighbour, and every one saying to his brother be of good courage; the carpenter encouraging the goldsmith, and he that smoteth with the hammer him that smote the anvil, saying: It is ready for the soldering and the fastening of nails."

---

*This is a grand idea, and not to be classed as practical in the utilitarian sense. Such a movement would appeal to all the finer and higher feelings of the citizens.—*Halifax Herald.*

We certainly wish the scheme every measure of success; it is practical, and we should think necessary, in a City like St. John, which is so representative of culture, enterprise and refinement.—*Quebec Chronicle.*

"It is now nearly a century since that patriotic band of men left their all for a home in British land, and came hither to build up what has become a prosperous commonwealth, and it has seemed that for nearly a hundred years nothing but the opportunity was wanting to bring into full play those noble sentiments of our people that have lingered ready to show by some spontaneously generous act their love for the memory of the founders of the country."—*St. John Common Council,* 1882.

St. John and Portland.

The centennial of the City should be celebrated by the union of St. John with Portland. The former, instead of ranking the seventh city of the Dominion, should be fourth, in the prestige of which Portland would share. The isolation of a century has worked to the injury of both.

The Farmers and the Centennial.

In no way can the farmers of New Brunswick better honor the memory of its founders than in setting out fruit and other trees, thus keeping green the incidents of a century, doing good to themselves, as well as to those who come after.

Arrival of the Fall Fleet.

The 4th of October, 1883, will be the 100th anniversary of the arrival of the fall fleet from New York in the harbor of the St. John River. This would be a fitting day to open the Dominion Exhibition, and lay the corner stone of a passenger depôt worthy a railway ere long to span the Continent; honored, it is hoped, by the presence of Her Royal Highness the Princess Louise and the Governor General.

The Army of Canada.

The interest in the Exhibition would be increased if the Dominion Army camped on the heights of Carleton, overlooking the historic ground where stood " Fort Latour," and where, in 1665, Lady Latour died.

On the Carleton heights stands the " Martello Tower," erected during the war of 1812. In proximity is "Fort Dufferin," at Negro Point. Should the exigencies of the country ever call for a Naval Academy, or the removal of the Military Academy to the seaboard, the historic ground of Carleton has strong claims for selection.

The North American Fleet and the Centennial.

Her Majesty Queen Victoria would do a graceful act to the memory of the men of 1783, as well as to the United States, to-

order the squadron on the North American station to St. John
during the Exhibition season, and join Fort Dufferin in a salute
to the "American Flag," for the honor done the British the 16th
October, 1881, on the historic field of Yorktown.

Of that day, an American wrote: "Beyond the famous field
of history — the field of the cloth of gold — will be the renown of
the plain of Yorktown. For there, when France and the United
States, with the friendly aid of a German veteran, stood in hostile array against England, on the hundredth anniversary of the
battle, the flags of France, Germany, England and the United
States floated gracefully together, hostile no longer. *Finis coro-
nat opus.* The salutation of the English flag at Yorktown was
the noble and worthy crown of all the long series of centennial
revolutionary celebrations. It was the symbol of the extinction
of the traditional enmity of the two countries, an earnest of that
federation of the world to which the hope and faith of Christen-
dom forever points."

Actions like these are hostages of peace, and do more to
cement friendship than Treaties or Acts of Parliament.

May the press of New Brunswick, as with a bugle blast, call
on the North, to give up; to the South, keep not back. Let
the sons and the daughters of New Brunswick from far and near
come in 1883 on a pilgrimage to the graves of their fathers — the
home of their childhood, for in this auspicious year in New
Brunswick history—

> "Something remains for all to do or dare ;
> Even the oldest tree some fruit may bear,
> For age is opportunity no less,
> Than youth itself, though in another dress ;
> And as the evening twilight fades away,
> The sky is filled with stars invisible by day."

CROWNING OF THE CENTENNIAL COLUMN.

As the 100th Anniversary of the last of the Loyalists leaving
New York, and the flag of England floating over the old thirteen
Colonies the last time, will be Sunday, 25th November, 1883,

D

there should be commemorative sermons, of a century surpassing in material progress the eighteen preceding ones.

" *Its days should speak, and multitude of years teach wisdom.*"

As the curtain drops on its last minutes, and two centuries blend in one, let there go forth as the voice of many waters to the tune of OLD HUNDRED, "A song in the night as when a holy solemnity is kept:"

> " Praise God from whom all blessings flow :
> Praise Him all creatures here below ;
> Praise Him above, ye heavenly host,
> Praise Father, Son, and Holy Ghost."

As the young men and maidens, old men and children, return to their homes in that historic midnight hour — memorable in Colonial history — may the chimes of " Trinity Church" peal forth JUBILEE notes of PEACE and GOOD WILL. "For the earth is the Lord's and the fulness thereof, the world and they that dwell therein." He alone can crown the CENTENNIAL with His goodness, and cause " the clouds to drop fatness ; to drop upon the dwellings of the wilderness, and make the little hills rejoice on every side ; make our garners full and plenteous with all manner of store, and our sheep bring forth thousands and ten thousands in our streets. Make our oxen strong to labor, that there be no decay, no going out, and no complaining in our streets. Happy are the people who are in such a case ; *yea,* blessed are the people who have the LORD for their GOD."

The reading of the paper was followed by Mr. A. A. Stockton, one of the Vice-Presidents, calling upon Chief Justice Allen, a grandson of one of the first Judges.

Chief Justice Allen spoke briefly. He thought that all must agree that it was a duty to do something to celebrate the landing of the Loyalists. There was but little time to do it now, and he trusted some one would take the matter in hand. No one was more capable of doing this work than Mr. Lawrence. He was full of knowledge in regard to the history of the Province, and most of his time was devoted to the work of historical research. He was preparing a book on the early judges and lawyers of the Province which he hoped soon to see in the press. He felt certain this work would be read with great interest. He had had the good fortune to hear some of the chapters of Mr. Lawrence's book read. He trusted that the very able and interesting paper which had just been read would be published, in order that every man in the Province should be able to see what the early history of St. John was.

Judge King also spoke. He had been much interested in Mr. Lawrence's paper. The circumstances connected with the early history of St. John were of great interest to us, who had been born in St. John or had come from other places to live here. He had been born in St. John, and the smallest details of its early history had great value to him. The more we can connect the people of the place with its local traditions and history the better it will be for us all. Any thing which tends to draw people together strengthens them. In a new country like this we lose a great deal that old countries possess, and therefore the labor of a Society like this does a substantial good. He closed by expressing his interest in the prosperity of the Society.

Senator Boyd, on being called on, made a short speech. He thanked the President for his interesting paper. He paid a high compliment to Judge King and also to Mayor Jones. The Hon. Josiah Jones, who was buried in Weymouth, was the grand-uncle of the Mayor. He, himself, was not a son of the Loyalists, but in no Loyalist's veins did more loyal blood run than in his. It was settled that the Dominion Exhibition of 1883 would be in St. John, and the grand railway terminus for St. John would be opened the same year. While so much was being said about the Northwest, he wanted to see more interest taken in the Northeast. We want before the centennial year a full history of St. John, got up by Mr. Lawrence and published by the citizens of St. John, and we must have an oration from Mr Lawrence on that centennial occasion. He concluded by moving a vote of thanks to Mr. Lawrence for his admirable paper, which was seconded by the Mayor, and carried unanimously.*

Mr. Elder, after thanking the chairman for his invitation to be present, spoke in praise of his eloquent and stirring address, and joined in the wish that it may be spread broadcast over the Province to stir up all to do their part towards the approaching Centennial. Though not a Loyalist, he felt that the terms Canadian and Loyalist were identical, and that all true Canadians would throw themselves into the celebration. He enlarged on the importance of the history of a country being preserved and cherished. It was not mere physical attractions, however grand, that endeared a people to a country; it was the association of deeds of human interest with portions of the earth; when such deeds were done they should be made to live on the page of history. He felt that the Historical Society was doing well to take up this matter, although the time was short. But if the gentlemen present here would throw their energies into this matter they could do much to achieve success. The programme which had been presented was an extensive one, but it was well to aim high, and what the Province failed to do the City would probably make

* The orator of the 18th of May, should be one eminently representative, as Hon. Sir Samuel Leonard Tilley, K. C. B., Minister of Finance and M. P. for the City of St. John; Hon. R. D. Wilmot, Lieut.-Governor, or the Hon. John C. Allen, Chief Justice of New Brunswick.

up. He heartily seconded the remarks of Senator Boyd—that a history of St. John should be written. He hoped that all would co-operate to make the Centennial a success, and to place St. John, which ought to be the fourth city of Canada, in a proper position before the world.

Mayor Jones said he feared he had got into a mutual admiration society. The reason Senator Boyd had piled it on to the Joneses was that he owned one of them; he was praising his wife over his (the Mayor's) shoulders. He greatly admired the paper read by the President; it should be published in proper form and he would aid in doing it. He would do all he could, both as a citizen and a member of the Common Council, to further the interests of the Society and of the proposed Centennial celebration.

Mr. D. S. Kerr on being called upon, thanked Mr. Lawrence for the very able address he had given. He was the son of a Loyalist, here he had settled, and here he was determined to die. Whatever he could do to forward the purpose the Society had in view he would do. New Brunswick was a country possessing great advantages. There was no portion of America with greater. Referring to the New Brunswick Society, he only regretted that the objects of the Society had not been carried out. He hailed with joy the discovery that there was still a living sentiment here in favor of the Loyalists. He regretted the lack of taste and regard for outside appearance in this Province. He concluded by saying that something must be done to keep our people in the country, and lamented that we had lost so many of our people already.

Mr. John Sears said that the present was one of the most pleasant social gatherings he had ever attended. The paper read was of great interest and must have involved a great deal of research. It was very desirable that from 2,000 to 3,000 copies of the paper should be published. Some of the facts mentioned in the paper were in his recollection. He remembered the coronation of George IV. and the roasting of the oxen on the square. This Loyalist celebration is one that should be taken part in by all citizens whether of Loyalist descent or not. He referred to the strong feelings which had been created by the war, now softened by time, but the acts of the Loyalists deserved recognition. He would like to see the President of the Society better paid for his labor than merely by thanks. He would like to see a resolution passed for the publication of the paper and a subscription opened to that end at the proper time.

Senator Boyd said that the Governor General, as soon as he returned from England, intended to establish a Literary Association, and historical research might be affiliated with it. Should this be done, and Mr. Lawrence put forward as the representative of the Society, he could be placed in a position where his useful historical labors would be properly rewarded.

Dr. Botsford hoped to see the interest which was now being manifested taking actual shape and form, and going beyond mere words. He expressed his strong sympathy with the objects and aims of the Society.

This closed the proceedings of the evening, which were of a very interesting character, and produced a most favorable impression on all who had the good fortune to be present.

ABRAHAM DePEYSTER.

His ancestors held a high position in France during the days of Huguenot persecution, when they fled to Holland. From there Johannes DePeyster came to New York the middle of the seventeenth century. The DePeysters from the first have been distinguished in New York city for wealth and character. When the war broke out, 1775, they sided with the Crown, and their property was confiscated. Abraham DePeyster, at the battle of King's Mountain, 1780, was a Captain in the 4th or King's American Regiment. In 1783 he was a grantee at Parr Town, having, shortly before leaving New York, married Catherine, a daughter of John Livingston, Esq. On the organization, 1785, of New Brunswick into Counties, Col. DePeyster was appointed Sheriff of Sunbury. On the retirement, 1792, of Richard Seaman from the Province Treasuryship, Col. DePeyster succeeded him, and removed to St. John. In February, 1798, he died, at the age of 45 years. His residence was on Prince William Street, the first north of the late Royal Hotel, opposite the Custom House, afterwards the residence of Thomas Wetmore, Esq.

As the relatives of Mrs. DePeyster were in New York, she removed there with her family on the death of her husband. Among the relics taken was the "Piano," appraised at ten pounds. The heirs on the male side of Col. DePeyster are all dead.

"*Dear Sir,*— "MAUGERVILLE, 10th July, 1792.

"I thank you for your answer to mine of the 27th ult., and its contents.

"At a meeting of our Church Wardens and Vestry, it was agreed that Mr. Daniels should be employed to make a ball, and Mr. Clarke to make a spindle and weathercock for our steeple, to be put up before the Right Reverend's visitation here, which we expect will be the last of this or the beginning of next month.

"It was also concluded in Vestry to secure the steeple against the rain, for which purpose is wanted a barrel of tar and 10 lbs. of oakum.

"We are likewise in want of a two quart pewter christening basin, two plates and a pint cup for our communion table, as

they will be required by the Bishop.   If the cup could be had of
block tin I should prefer it.

"These, if you will be so good as to procure, and charge to
the Church account, and send them by the first opportunity, and
engage the boatman, whoever he is, to be punctual in leaving
them at my house, it will much oblige your friends here, and
none more so than, dear Sir,

"Your most obedient, humble servant,

"JOHN BEARDSLEY.*

"COLONEL DEPEYSTER.

"N. B.—Family compliments wait on Mrs. DePeyster and
the dear children."

A PURCHASE OF TWO SLAVES BY ABRAHAM DEPEYSTER AT ST. JOHN.

"*Know all men by these Presents,* That I, Munson Jarvis, of
the city of St. John, New Brunswick, for and in consideration
of Sixty Pounds to me in hand paid, on and before the sealing
and delivery of these Presents, by Abraham DePeyster, of said
city and Province aforesaid, the receipt whereof I do hereby
acknowledge, have bargained, sold, and by these Presents do
bargain, sell and deliver unto him, the said Abraham DePeyster,
one negro man named Abraham, and one negro woman named
Lucy.   I, the said Munson Jarvis, my heirs and assigns, from
and against all persons shall and will warrant and defend by
these Presents, the said negro man and negro woman.

"In witness whereof, I have hereunto set my hand and seal
the fifteenth day of July, 1797.   In presence of us.

"JOHN WARD.   "MUNSON JARVIS.
"R. M. JARVIS."

The Loyalists were dependent for help on slaves, or others
of color.

---

* Rev. John Beardsley was a grantee of Parr Town.   He married a daughter of Bartholomew Crannell, the first Common Clerk of St. John.   After the
death of Rev. John Sayre, 1784, he succeeded him as Rector of Maugerville.
In the war, he was Chaplain of Col. Beverley Robinson's Regiment.   He died
at Kingston, King's County, 1810, where he resided from 1802, receiving a
pension from the British Government.

A SLAVE IN COURT.

In 1800, a test case was before the Bench, Fredericton; George Duncan Ludlow, Chief Justice; Judges Allen, Upham, and Saunders.

Counsel for the Master:	Counsel for the Slave:
Jonathan Bliss,	Ward Chipman,
Thomas Wetmore,	Samuel Denny Street.
John Murray Bliss,	
Charles J. Peters,	
William Botsford.	

All the Counsel addressed the Court. The speech of Jonathan Bliss was divided into thirty-two heads. Ward Chipman's covers eighty pages of foolscap. The two are extant, as well as correspondence on the question between Chief Justice Blowers of Nova Scotia and the latter. The Bench divided, the Chief Justice and Judge Upham supported the Master's right; Judge Allen and Judge Saunders decided against the sufficiency of the return. As no judgment was entered, the master took back his slave. From this time, slave property depreciated, some masters entering into an agreement for a fixed period on wages.

One result of the trial was a challenge from Stair Agnew to Judge Allen to fight a duel, carried by John Murray Bliss. The challenge was not accepted; at that time a more courageous act than to fight. Agnew and Bliss were indicted.

Consequent on some words spoken at the trial, Agnew* and S. Denny Street† (one of the Counsel for the slave), fought.

---

*Stair Agnew was a Captain in the Queen's Rangers. His residence in New Brunswick was opposite Fredericton, where he died, 1821, aged 63 years. For over 25 years he was one of the members for York.

†Samuel Denny Street, in 1781, was on service at Fort Howe, mouth of St. John River. At the organization of the Courts, he was admitted to the Bar, and settled in Sunbury County. He was the father of William H., John Ambrose, George Frederick and Denny Lee Street. He died 11th December, 1830, in his 79th year.

On leaving Court at Fredericton, words passed between George Frederick Street and George Ludlow Wetmore, which led to a challenge. The seconds were Lieut. R. Davis, of 74th Regt., and John H. Winslow. They met on

They were indicted, with their seconds, Bliss and Anderson.
Neither of the indictments came to trial; they stood over, and
were ultimately quashed for irregularity.

At the St. John Circuit, September, 1798, Judge Allen * on
the Bench, Luke Hamilton, a slave of Judge Upham,† was tried
for the murder of the girl West. Luke was returning on horseback to the residence of his master, Hammond River, when he

---

Maryland Hill, Oct. 2nd, 1821. Shots were exchanged, when Mr. Wetmore
was struck in the head and only survived a few hours. An offer of £30 was
made for the apprehension of Messrs. Street, Davis and Winslow, or £10 for
any one of them. They went to Robinstown, opposite St. Andrews, and after
a few months returned to Fredericton and gave themselves up. The 22nd of
February, 1822, they were tried before Judge Saunders, with Solicitor General
Botsford prosecuting officer. As the evidence was unable to identify positively the prisoners, the Jury through their foreman, Mark Needham, brought
in a verdict of not guilty.

* Judge Allen, at close of war, was Col. of 2nd Battalion N. J. Volunteers.
On his appointment to the Bench of New Brunswick, with a seat in the Council, he obtained a grant of 2,000 acres, above Fredericton, 500 being an Island,
called "Isle Sauvage," in the St. John River, which had been granted some
years before to Francis Xavier and three other Indian Chiefs, for the use of the
Milicite Tribe. The place was called "Aukpaque," or "Okpaha," beginning of
swift water, or head of tide. Judge Allen purchased from the Indians their interest in the Island. The first Baptist preacher at Fredericton was one known
in later years as Father Manning. Judge Allen was asked for a warrant for his
arrest. His answer was, "I will hear him for myself." The Judge, unable
to get into the house, stood outside, unknown to Mr. Manning. The text was,
"Behold the Judge standeth at the door." After service, he said to those who
asked for the warrant: "God forbid I should lay hands on that young man. I
would there were more like him in the country." The Judge died 1806, aged
65 years. His son John, for over 25 years one of the members for York, died
29th April, 1875, aged 91 years. The old homestead at "Aukpaque" is in
possession of the grandson of the Judge, the Hon. John C. Allen, Chief Justice of New Brunswick.

† Judge Upham was a Massachusetts Loyalist, and at the close of the war
Major in the Dragoons. His residence in New Brunswick was at Hammond
River. At the organization of the Province he was a member of the Council
and one of the Bench. In 1806, at the request of his brother Judges, he went
to England to ask an increase of salary, from £300 to £500 stg. In this he
was successful. On the eve of returning, he died, November 1, 1808, at the
age of 67 years. A daughter of the Judge was the first wife of the Hon. John
W. Weldon.

met the girl picking berries, two miles from the city, near the Old Westmorland Road. He was convicted from the marks on the ground of the horse-shoes, near where the body of the girl was found. Luke was executed.

First Ejectment Trial in New Brunswick.

The Governor of Nova Scotia made a grant to Bryan Finucane, Chief Justice of that Province, only a month before New Brunswick was formed, of "Sugar Island," eight miles above Fredericton, on the River St. John,—an island of 500 acres. In 1785, the Chief Justice died, when his brother Andrew claimed it, as heir at law. The Island at this time was divided into 10 acre lots, held by disbanded troops.

"Halifax, March 27, 1785.

" *My dear Chipman:*

"The Chief Justice's grant of Sugar Island was indisputably included in the general location of land to the Provincials, drawn for, and in the actual possession of particular corps, and under the sanction and permission of the Governor of Nova Scotia. Integrity blushes at the recollection of it and other grants, and the most intrepid friend to Government will shudder at the contemplation of such iniquity. . . . . . I hope Col. Allen and all the parties will dispute it by inches.

"Your's,   Edw. Winslow."

"Fredericton, 6th July, 1786.

" *Dear Sir:*

"Mr. A. Finucane has arrived: what reception he will meet with I cannot at present understand. Col. Allen has publicly expressed himself, 'That he will not receive him at his table, as the character he appears in is so disagreeable to all ranks of people in this part of York. Of this he will inform him when he meets him. Should Mr. Finucane venture, in *propria persona*, upon the premises, to display his courage, it may chance to be cooled by a species of discipline ill suited to his years.'

"Thus much for Sugar Island, *Gu-enim* Island; the latter would be an excellent substitute for an Indian name, and would afford an admirable opportunity for some future New Brunswick antiquarian to prove the affinity between the Latin and the Indian language. Mr. Finucane has just published a flaming advertisement, forbidding all depredations or improvements on Sugar Island, as the offenders will be prosecuted as the law directs. 'Bravo,' Mr. Finucane. Col. Allen says, '*Bravissimo*.'"

"Your most obedient,

"WARD CHIPMAN, Esq."   "JONATHAN SEWELL, Jun.

FINUCANE *vs*. STELLE.

The trial came on at Fredericton, 1787. On the bench, Chief Justice Ludlow, Judges Putnam and Upham ; Counsel for the Plaintiff, Jonathan Bliss and Elias Hardy ; for the Defendant, William Wylly * and Ward Chipman. The Plaintiff was non-suited.

Ward Chipman wrote Judge Allen on the eve of the trial :

"There occurs to me after the laborious task I have had in investigating this business, a good old adage which, reversed, will stand thus : *Qui sentit onus sentire et comodium.* If we can get rid of this iniquitous grant, I think we should have something for our trouble, and that we shall is, beyond every doubt, certain.   "Adieu, my dear Sir,

"Your most devoted friend
and humble servant,

"W. CHIPMAN."

THE FIRST APPEAL CASE.

At the February Term, 1793, Finucane brought an action for Ejectment from Sugar Island against Frederick DePeyster ; Judges Upham and Saunders on the bench. Elias Hardy for Plaintiff ; Ward Chipman for Defendant.

---

* William Wylly was a Southern loyalist, and the first King's Counsel and Registrar of Court of Vice-Admiralty in New Brunswick. Mrs. Wylly was a daughter of Mr. Mathews, the last Mayor of New York, under the Crown. In 1787, Mr. Wylly left with his family for the Bahamas, and the year after was Solicitor General and Surrogate of Court of Vice-Admiralty. In 1804 Mr. Wylly was appointed Advocate General of Vice-Admiralty Court. In 1812 he was Chief Justice, and exchanged in 1814 with the Attorney General. In 1822 he was appointed Chief Justice of St. Vincent. Mr. Wylly died in Devonshire, Eng., 1828, aged 71 years, leaving four sons and four daughters.

Fred? de Peyster

The evidence of Michael Finucane, father of the Plaintiff, taken under a commission in Ireland, to prove the heirship of Andrew, was offered in evidence, and objected to as inadmissible, as the father was an interested party, being next of kin to the Plaintiff. Judge Upham thought it admissible, Judge Saunders *contra;* it, however, was received. Mr. DePeyster's Counsel tendered a bill of exceptions to the ruling of the Court, and brought a writ of error, which was argued before the Court of Appeals (the Governor and Council), which reversed the judgment of the Court. Finucane appealed to the King in Council from the judgment of the Court of Errors; its judgment was sustained, and the occupants of Sugar Island retained possession.

AARON BURR ON SUGAR ISLAND.

"*Sir:*   "NEW YORK, 28th May, 1794.

"I have perused with much pleasure the cause of Finucane and DePeyster which you transmitted to me at Philadelphia. It has not been in my power, by reason of pressing public engagements, to examine attentively the authorities, much less to attempt any further elucidation of the subject. Indeed, the industry and ability displayed by the Defendant's Counsel leave little room to hope that new light can be thrown upon it.

"I am clearly in opinion with the Court of Errors in their reversal of the judgment of the Supreme Court, and think that the cause before the King in Council may, on the part of the Defendant, be safely trusted to the arrangement and authorities contained in the case you have submitted to my perusal.

"I am, respectfully, dear Sir,
"Your humble servant,

"Capt. DEPEYSTER."   *Aaron Burr*

Frederic DePeyster, a brother of Abraham, at the close of the war, was a Captain in the King's 3rd American Regiment. In swimming a river on horseback, a rifle bullet passed through both legs, killing his horse. In 1783 he was a grantee of Parr Town. He shortly after removed to the County of York, of which he was a Magistrate. In 1792, he was at New York, engaged in business.

Captain DePeyster was so thin when in the British service, that not one of his sons, when grown up, could get on his uniform coat, and when sixty was so large there were few such to be met. His first wife was a daughter of Commissary General Hake; his second, a daughter of Gerard G. Beckman, and granddaughter of Lieut.-Governor Van Cortlandt. Capt. DePeyster died of apoplexy, 1830, aged 70 years. He walked from his tea table to his death-bed, having never had a pain nor an ache in his lifetime, throughout which he never touched a drop of spirits. He never renounced his allegiance to the British Crown.

His son, Frederic, died at his country seat, Duchess County, New York, 18th August, 1882, in his 86th year, leaving a son, Gen. J. Watts DePeyster, noted for his interest in historic matters.

In the Southern rebellion three great grandsons of Frederic DePeyster, a grantee of Parr Town, took part; two died from exposure in the war. Johnston DePeyster (now Col.) hoisted, 3rd April, 1865, the first Union flag on the Capitol of Richmond. The Christmas following, the city of New York tendered to him (then in his 18th year) the thanks of the city for giving New York this historic honor.

The descendants of Abraham and Frederic DePeyster to-day hold a first place in New York.

THE MALLARD HOUSE

was a plain two story building, on the North side of King Street, where the Royal Hotel stands. At the first election of members for the House of Assembly, it was the head-quarters of the Government candidates—Jonathan Bliss, Ward Chipman, Christopher Billop,* William Pagan, Stephen Hoyt, John McGeorge.

---

* Col. Billop, when the war commenced, was a member of the New York Legislature, representing Staten Island, where he resided, and Colonel of the Militia. The following is an incident in his history:

" To the Keeper of the Common Jail for the County of Burlington. Greeting:
"You are hereby commanded to receive into your custody the body of Colonel Christopher Billop, prisoner of war, herewith delivered to you, and

The card of the candidates closed as follows: " If we have the honor to be elected, we will not directly nor indirectly, receive any pay, reward, gratuity or allowance for our time, or attendance, or service as representatives in the General Assembly."

The poll opened Monday, the 7th of November, 1785. In the first issue of the *Royal Gazette** after, was the following:]

having put irons on his hands and feet, you are to chain him down to the floor in a close room in the said jail, and there to detain him, giving him bread and water only for food, until you receive further orders from me, or the Commissary of Prisoners for the State of New Jersey.

" Given under my hand at Eliz'th Town, this 6th day of November, 1779.

" ELISHA BOUDINOT, Commissioner Pris., New Jersey.

" SIR,—Sorry I am that I have been put under the disagreeable necessity of a treatment towards your person that will prove so irksome to you; but retaliation is directed, and it will, I most sincerely hope, be in your power to relieve yourself from relaxation of the sufferings of John Leshier. It seems nothing short of retaliation will teach Britons to act like men of humanity.

" I am, Sir, your most humble servant,
" To COL. CHRISTOPHER BILLOP." " ELISHA BOUDINOT, Com. Prisoners.

John Leshier had murdered a Loyalist, whom he had waylaid. In 1797, Col. Billop was appointed to a seat in the Council. The Hon. Wm. Black, and the Rev. Dr. Willis, Rector of Trinity, married daughters. His residence was in King Street, the next below the present Waverley House. Col. Billop died in his 90th year, 28th March, 1827.

* Christopher Sower was born at Germantown, near Philadelphia, January 27th, 1754, and worked at the business of printing. From 1778 to the close of the war he was in New York. At the evacuation he went to London to get compensation. In addition to an allowance in money, he was granted a pension, with the offices of Deputy Postmaster General and King's Printer of New Brunswick. Mr. Sower arrived in the Province in the fall of 1784. The first printing office, with the post office, was in Dock Street. In 1790, Mr. Sower bought of Monsieur Tabideau and others, at French Village, Hammond River, 1,400 acres of land. He named his place "Brookville" (now Government Stock Farm). Mr. Sower built a two-story double log house for his residence and printing office. The *Royal Gazette* and Journals of the Legislature were printed at Brookville. At the election, 1792, Mr. Sower was an unsuccessful candidate. In the spring of 1799, he went on a visit to Philadelphia and Baltimore, and had completed arrangements with his brother Samuel for a co-partnership in a type foundry, when he was stricken with apoplexy, and died July 3rd, 1799, at the age of 43 years, leaving a widow, one son and four daughters. The son, Brook Watson Sower, learned the business of printer with his uncle at Philadelphia. He died in Virginia

E

"Wednesday evening last, a mob collected at McPherson's Coffee House, where the poll had been held the first two days, and proceeded a little after dark, armed with sticks, clubs and bludgeons, to Mallard's, where a number were quietly and peacefully collected. The mob, after the most violent threats against those who were in the house, wounded several gentlemen who defended the passage at the door, and made a general attack upon the house with stones and brick-bats, demolishing all the windows. The gentlemen within, fearing immediate destruction to themselves, returned the stones and brick-bats upon the mob, who began to grow very violent and outrageous. By this means, and the seasonable interposition of the troops from Fort Howe in aid of the civil magistrate, the mob was dispersed. Several that were concerned were apprehended and confined.

"The rioters were admitted to bail for their appearance at the next Supreme Court, and in the meantime to keep the peace and be of good behaviour.

"A number of merchants and others met at Mallard's immediately after, to consult on the best means of continuing the election. Attorney General Bliss, in a speech of considerable length, clearly stated the present position of public affairs, and the necessity of making choice of proper persons to represent the City and County of St. John in the General Assembly; he took notice of the unjust clamor raised against the agents for the location of lands and distribution of supplies, and others in whom the Government have confidence."

The poll continued to the end of fifteen days, when the Government candidates were elected.

TRIAL OF THE RIOTERS.

A Supreme Court of Judicature opened at St. John 2nd May, 1786.

On the Bench:* The Hon. George Duncan Ludlow, *Chief Justice;* Hon. James Putnam, Hon. Isaac Allen, *Puisne Judges.*

1866, at the age of 82. A son and namesake is living in Philadelphia, the oldest representative of the first King's Printer and first Deputy Postmaster General of New Brunswick.

* When two or more Judges sat on the Bench, it was called "Trial at Bar." The last at St. John was in 1788. They were continued at Fredericton many years. When the Judges differed, each charged the Jury.—*From Manuscript:* "Early Lawyers and Judges of New Brunswick and their Times."

The leading rioters—John Jenkins, John Mullin, Jeremiah Cane, William Reily, James Higgins, and Charles McConnell—were placed on trial.

Sheriff Oliver, one of the witnesses on the part of the Crown, said:

"After the poll for the day was over at Carleton, went to McPherson's; the house was full. At dusk, saw a great number at the the corner with clubs, crying, 'let us go up.' Dissuaded them; they appeared quiet; afterwards endeavored to quiet the mob at Mallard's; told them he was the Sheriff, and commanded peace, but to no purpose; the brick-bats drove them off; they endeavored to rally; said they lost Tool; endeavored to get him out."

The Jury returned Jenkins, Reily and Higgins guilty, on which they were fined Ten Pounds each, with three months imprisonment to Reily and Higgins, and to find security in Fifty Pounds each for their good behaviour for three months, and to stand committed until their fines and fees were paid.

The 3rd day of January, 1786, the first Session of the Legislature met at the Mallard House.

MEMBERS ELECTED.

St. John: William Pagan, Jonathan Bliss, Christopher Billop, Ward Chipman, John McGeorge, Stanton Hazard.

York: Daniel Murray, Isaac Atwood, Daniel Lyman, Edward Stelle.

Westmorland: Amos Botsford, Charles Dixon, Samuel Gay, Andrew Kinnear.

King's: John Coffin, Ebenezer Foster.

Queen's: Samuel Dickinson, John Yeomans.

Charlotte: William Paine, James Campbell, Robert Pagan, Peter Clinch.

Northumberland: Elias Hardy, William Davidson.

Sunbury: William Hubbard, Richard Vandeburg.

Speaker: Amos Botsford; *Clerk:* William Paine.

The returns were made to the Provincial Secretary * by the following Sheriffs:

---

* Hon. and Rev. Jonathan Odell, through the war, was Chaplain to a loyal New Jersey Regiment. In 1782, colors were presented to the King's Ameri-

St. John: Wm. S. Oliver; *York:* John Murray; *Westmorland:* Ambrose Sherman; *King's:* Crosby Hunt; *Queen's:* John Robinson; *Northumberland:* Benjamin Marsten; *Charlotte:* Thomas Wyer; *Sunbury:* Abraham DePeyster.

First Dramatic Performance in New Brunswick!

FOR PUBLIC CHARITY,

On Saturday, 28th of March, 1789,

AT MALLARD'S LONG ROOM, KING STREET,

will be performed,

THE COMEDY OF

THE BUSY BODY!

To which will be added:

WHO'S THE DUPE?

"The doors to be opened at *half-past Five.* To begin precisely at half-past Six o'clock.

"Tickets at three shillings each, to be had at MALLARD'S.

"No money will be received at the door, nor any person admitted without Ticket."

"*Editorial.*—Saturday evening last, was presented before the most numerous and polite assembly which has appeared in this Town, 'The Busy Body,' with 'Who's the Dupe?' by a company of Gentlemen. Mallard's Long Room on this occasion was converted into a pretty Theatre. The scenes, the decorations and dresses were entirely new, and in a very fine style. The parts of the Drama were, in general, well cast, and the characters supported with great life and humor. Some * of the Company displayed comic talents which

---

can Dragoons at New York, in the presence of Prince William Henry, when Mr. Odell delivered an address. At the organization of New Brunswick, he was appointed Provincial Secretary, with a seat in Council. Mr. Odell died at Fredericton, 25th of November, 1818, in his 82nd year. He was the last of the Council of 1784. His son, William Franklin, named after the last loyal Governor of New Jersey, was born there, 1776. He studied law in the office of Ward Chipman. To him the honor belongs of designating MARS HILL, the N. W. angle of Nova Scotia. In the office of Provincial Secretary he succeeded his father. He died November 25th, 1844, at the age of 68 years. The chief representative to-day is Hon. William H. Odell, one of New Brunswick's Senators.

* At a performance at the Bristol Grammar School, England, Jonathan and Stephen Sewell took part. One of the tragedians present was Mrs. Sid-

would have done honor to a British Theatre; and it is justice to say that all
exceeded the expectations of the most favourable of their friends. The ap-
plauses of the assembly manifested the highest gratification in this the first
dramatic exhibition in this Province."

PROLOGUE.

      ※   *   ※   ※

Here, too, in honored loyalty's retreat,
Where citizens from every clime have met,
Distress is found — distress that knows belief —
Distress that asks, and that requires relief.

    ※   *   *   ※   ※   ※

A humane band of citizens, 'tis true,
Have done much good, but much is yet to do;
Their scanty fund with conscious joy we know
Hath oft relieved variety of woe.

Their reverend Patron, who with steady zeal
Urged every measure for the public weal ;
Too soon they lost — in early age he fled,
With all the honors of a hoary head.
His words, *his* actions, with peculiar charm,
Made selfish vice the liberal pleasures try,
And stoics owe the glow of charity.

  *   *   *   *   *   ※

---

dons. She was so much pleased with Jonathan that she sent to him the
following complimentary lines from her pen:

"The world is dull, and seldom gives us cause
For joy, surprise or well deserved applause;
Young Heaven-taught Sewell;* behold! in thee
Sufficient cause for all the three.
Thy rising genius managed Cato's part
To charm away and captivate the heart;
'Tis rare for boys like thee to play the man—
There are but few in years who nobly can ;
But thou, a youth of elegance and ease,
In Cato's person, to perform and please,
Hast common youth and manhood both outdone,
And proved thyself dame nature's chosen son."

---

*Jonathan Sewell, in 1808, was Chief Justice of Quebec. In 1838 he
resigned on a pension from the British Government of £1,000 stg. He was
born at Boston, June 6th, 1766, and died at Quebec, November 12th, 1839.
Mrs. Sewell, a daughter of William Smith, the last Chief Justice of New York
under the Crown, and the first of Quebec, died at the age of 74 years, 29th
May, 1849. Of 22 children, 12 survived her.

BENEDICT ARNOLD.

Benedict Arnold, on joining the British service at New York, 1780, received six thousand guineas, with the command of a regiment and the rank of a General. In January, 1781, he was in command of the forces at Virginia, remaining there until his return in June to New York. He was succeeded by Lord Cornwallis, who, on the 19th of October, surrendered to General Washington.

From the "Chesapeake" prize money Arnold received £2,068.

On the 15th of December, 1781, Arnold left New York for England with a fleet of one hundred sail. He was on board the ship *Robust;* the other passengers in her were, Lord Cornwallis, Gen. Tarleton, Cols. Dundas, York and Lake, Major Ross and Capt. Sterling.

After being out eleven days, a gale arose, so violent that the *Robust* was so much injured that she had to bear away for the West Indies. Lord Cornwallis, with others, went on board the *Grey Hound,* and Gen. Arnold and Capt. Sterling on board the *Edward.* Arnold, after a residence in England of less than four years, returned to America. While there the British Government gave Mrs. Arnold a pension for life of £500 sterling, with pensions of £100 to each of her children.

"Dear CHIPMAN: "HALIFAX, Nov. 22, 1785.

. . . . . . "Will you believe General Arnold is here from England, in a brig of his own, as he says, reconoitering the country. He is bound for your city, which he will of course prefer to Halifax, and settle with you. Give you joy of the acquisition.   "S. S. BLOWERS."

Arnold arrived at St. John, and purchased lot 1329, Main Street, Lower Cove, and on it erected a store. In May, 1786, he purchased of Nehemiah Beckwith a vessel on the stocks at Maugerville, river St. John. He named her the "Lord Sheffield." Arnold went on a trading voyage to the West Indies in her, and from there to England, leaving his business at St. John with his partner, Munson Hayt. On the suggestion of his friends in

B. Arnold

England he effected insurance on the Lower Cove building of £1,000; on stock, £4,000; and on stock in the King Street store, £1,000 sterling.

Arnold returned to St. John in the ship *Peggy*, arriving there with his family July, 1787.

On the night of the 11th July, 1788, the Lower Cove store, with its contents, was burnt. The General's son, Henry, was sleeping there, and narrowly escaped with his life.

Nearly two years after the fire, Munson Hayt, from whom he had separated, charged Arnold with setting fire to the building, on which the General brought an action for slander, claiming £5,000 damages, retaining Attorney General Bliss and Solicitor General Chipman. Hayt's Counsel was Elias Hardy. The trial came on at the September Court, 1790, before Judge Allen and the following jury: Thomas Suvenor, Adam Henigar, Edwin Ewar, Daniel Leavitt, Stephen Humbert, Tredway F. Older, James Gaynor, Thomas Mullin, John Whitman, James Hart, William Clarke, Charles McPherson.

The jury gave the plaintiff twenty shillings damages.

BENEDICT ARNOLD LEAVES NEW BRUNSWICK.

"PUBLIC AUCTION, at the house of General Arnold, King Street, Thursday, 22nd September, at 11 o'clock, if fair weather, if not, the first fine day:

A QUANTITY OF HOUSEHOLD FURNITURE,

comprising excellent feather beds, mahogany four post bedsteads, with furniture; a set of elegant Cabriole chairs, covered with blue damask, sofas and curtains to match; Card, Tea and other Tables, looking glasses, a Secretary desk and book-case, fire screens, girandoles, lustres, an easy and sedan chair, with a great variety of other furniture.

"*Likewise:* An elegant set of Wedgewood Gilt Ware, two Tea table sets of Nankeen China, a variety of glassware, a Terrestrial Globe. Also a double Wheel Jack, and a great quantity of kitchen furniture. Also, a Lady's elegant Saddle and Bridle.

"JOHN CHALONER,

"*St. John, Sept. 6, 1791.*   "Auctioneer."

ARNOLD IN ENGLAND.

DUEL WITH LORD LAUDERDALE.

Of the duel, Mrs. Arnold wrote a son of the General's by his first wife:

"I was greatly distressed by your father being concerned in a duel; but it has ended so safely and honorable to him, I am happy it has taken place. The Earl of Lauderdale cast some reflections upon his public character in the House of Lords, for which your father demanded an apology, which his Lordship refused to make. On Sunday morning, July the first, they went out a few miles from London, with their seconds, Lord Hawke your father's, and Charles Fox Lord Lauderdale's. Lord Lauderdale received your father's fire, but refused to return it, saying he had no enmity to him. Your father, declared he would not quit the field without an apology. His Lordship made a very satisfactory one. Your father has gained very great credit in this business, and I fancy it will deter others from taking liberties with him."

"*Dear Sir*,—   "LONDON, August 16, 1792.

"We feel ourselves much obliged to you and Mrs. Chipman for the kindly concern you expressed for the sufferings on the voyage to England, and for your good wishes. We have the pleasure to assure you that we enjoy tolerable health, and find this country full as pleasant as St. John, though we much regret the loss of the little friendly society we had there.

"I have taken the liberty to send you a small parcel, containing flannel hose, socks and a pair of gloves, which I beg you to accept. Should you again be attacked with the gout, you will find them serviceable; I most sincerely wish it may be the case. I certainly would not, had I the power to transfer the disease to some of my *good friends at St. John*. There is a small parcel in your's that I will thank you to send to Mr. Bliss.

"Mrs. Arnold joins me in best wishes to you and Mrs. Chipman, and in sincere wishes for your health and happiness. Mas-

ter George* and Sophia unite in love to Master Chip.† We beg
to be remembered to Mr. Hazen's family.

                    "I am, with great regard,
                            "Dear Sir, yours,
"WARD CHIPMAN, Esq., St. John."   "B. ARNOLD.

                        "LONDON, 30th August, 1793.
"Dear Sir :
     "I intended writing by our friend Robert Parker,‡ but his
attention was so much taken up with the ladies when in Devonshire that he did not let any of his friends know when or where
he embarked. I hear he is married to a very pretty and agree-
able lady, and that they embarked in the August packet for
Halifax.
     "I hope soon to have the pleasure of hearing from you. I
received a letter from Jonathan Bliss, of July: he was then so
much elated and so happy on the birth of a second son§ that he
did not mention any news . . . . .
                    "Sincerely your's,   B. ARNOLD."

----

     * Master George was born at the King Street residence, St. John, Septem-
ber 5, 1787. He died November 1, 1828, in India, Lieut.-Col. in the Bengal
Cavalry. He was named George after George Washington, his father's early
friend, and George III., his later friend.

     † Master Chip. was born at St. John, July 10th, 1787. He died 26th
November, 1851, aged 64 years, having held a seat on the Bench nearly 27
years.

     ‡ Robert Parker was a Massachusetts Loyalist. On the peace, he was
appointed Comptroller of Customs and Ordnance Store-keeper at Saint John,
holding both offices to his death in 1823 at the age of 74 years. Mrs. Parker
died at the age of 84, October, 1852. Hon. Chief Justice Parker, who died at
St. John, Nov. 1865, aged 69 years, and Hon. Neville Parker, one of the
Judges of the Supreme Court, who died at St. Andrews, August, 1869, aged
71 years, were sons.

     § The son of Jonathan Bliss was Lewis, the donor of the Family Memorial
Window in the Chancel of Trinity Church, St. John. He was the last of the
four sons, and died 7th September, 1882, aged 89 years, and, with his brother
Henry, was buried in Kendal Green Cemetery, London.

GENERAL ARNOLD IN THE WEST INDIES.

"*Dear Sir:*   "MARTINIQUE, 14th Jan'y, 1795.

"A few days ago I had the pleasure of receiving letters from Jonathan Bliss and Ebenezer Putnam,* who informed me my friends are all well, among whom I rank you and Mr. Parker. You will all, no doubt, be glad to hear that, after the variety of scenes I have passed through in this country, and some of them very hazardous, I not only escaped, but am in the enjoyment of good health.

"You seem placed in a corner of the world where you are free from the alarms and misfortunes of war, which is a great blessing. I expect to embark for England in April, considerably improved in fortune and infinitely more in health than when I left England; and though I have experienced the distress of burying two-thirds of my acquaintances in these Islands since I came out, I scarcely had an hour's sickness.

"I hope you have been fortunate to collect the few debts of mine left with you, and remitted to Mrs. Arnold.

                              "Sincerely yours,
"WARD CHIPMAN, ESQ.,   "B. ARNOLD.

"*Dear Sir:*   "ST. PIERRE, MARTINIQUE, 4th May, 1795.

"I have been detained here longer than I expected, but hope to embark in few days for England. . . . . . . While I have made money in this country, I have lately met with a loss of nearly £3,000 at Grenada, which makes it necessary for me to collect as many of my old debts as possible. I beg you will presents my best respects to Mrs. Chipman and to all friends.

                    "I am, with great regard, your's,
"WARD CHIPMAN."   "B. ARNOLD.

---

* Ebenezer Putnam was the second son of Judge Putnam. He was a merchant at St. John, an Alderman and Registrar of Deeds. He died, 1798, at the age of 36. He left three sons: Francis, who died at St. Andrews, 1836, aged 39 years; Charles, who died at Fredericton, 1837; and John, who died at Boston. The representative of the family, John Millidge Putnam, a son of Charles, for many years has resided in England.

MRS. ARNOLD TO WARD CHIPMAN.

LONDON, Queen Ann's Street, East, }
4th June, 1795. }

"*Sir:*

"Mr. Robbins having sailed some time ago for America, I take the liberty of enclosing you the protest. The bill shall go through the regular form, and be returned to you to take proceedings. General Arnold is not yet returned to England, but I expect to see him in the course of a month. You have no doubt heard of the many wonderful escapes he has had, some of which could only have been effected by his uncommon exertions.

"With respect to politics, I am a miserable croaker, and ought not, perhaps, to touch them.

"The desertion of our allies places dear old England, in my opinion, in a very critical situation; and the late unpopular measure of bringing the Prince of Wales' debts before Parliament, added to the heavy taxes that must unavoidably be paid for the prosecution of the war, creates great uneasiness at home. But at present, we certainly could not make peace upon honorable terms.

"I hear much of the gaiety of your little city, but find party spirit, especially among the ladies, still rages with violence. I shall always regret my separation from many valuable friends, among the first of whom I shall always reckon Mrs. Chipman. Please have the goodness to make my best compliments to her, and believe me, with much esteem,

"Yours, &c., M. ARNOLD."

Their son, James Robertson Arnold, an officer in the Royal Engineers, was at St. John 1819. On visiting the old home, he wept as a child. In 1830 William IV. appointed him one of his aides-de-camp.

Benedict Arnold died at London, June 14, 1801, in his 62nd year. By his first wife he had two sons, Robert and Henry. They settled in Upper Canada on a grant from the British Government of 13,000 acres to their father in 1798 for his services at Guadeloupe.

General Arnold married, April 8, 1777, for his second wife, a daughter of Edward Shippen, the last Royal Attorney General of Pennsylvania. Mrs. Arnold died at London, 24th August, 1804, in her 45th year, leaving four sons and one daughter. Of her an American lately wrote: "In the difficult positions she occupied, as the wife of General Arnold, she bore herself with a dignity and grace, and with a modesty, sincerity and truth, of which any people might be justly proud."

THE FIRST RECTOR OF ST. JOHN.

The following Ecclesiastical intelligence is from the *Royal Gazette*, August 1, 1786: "Last Sunday morning the Rev. Geo. Bisset, lately arrived from England, preached in the *Church* in this City, and in the evening Messrs. Moore and Gibbons, of the people called Quakers, the former from New Jersey, the latter from Pennsylvania. The whole gave great satisfaction."

Mr. Bisset's ministry was short, for he died 3rd March, 1788, leaving a widow and one son. Before the war he was Rector of Trinity Church, Newport, Rhode Island.

The Church was on lot 121 Germain Street (east side), between Duke and Queen Streets, used also for the Court Rooms and Common Council Chambers.

The corner stone of "Old Trinity Church" was laid by the Right Rev. CHARLES,* Lord Bishop of Nova Scotia, 20th August, 1788, followed by a charge to the clergy and administration of confirmation to a large number.

The Rector of St. John at the opening of Trinity Church was Mather Byles, D.D.,† last Rector of Christ's Church, Bos-

---

* Rev. Charles Inglis, D.D., was the last Rector of New York under the Crown. In 1781-2 he was Chaplain to 1st Batt. New Jersey Volunteers. At evacuation, 1783, Dr. Inglis went to Halifax. In 1787 he went to England, and the 12th of August that year he was consecrated at Lambeth, the first Bishop of Nova Scotia, with jurisdiction over the other North American Provinces. He was the first Colonial Bishop of the Church of England. Dr. Inglis died at Halifax, 24th February, 1816, in the 82nd year of his age, 58th of his ministry, and 29th of his consecration.

† Dr. Byles died at St. John, 12th March, 1814, in his 80th year.

CHARLES INGLIS, D. D.

ton. In a report to the S. P. G. Society he wrote: "The new Church was opened Christmas Day, 1791, when he administered to sixty communicants, and on the following Easter to eighty. In the year he baptized fifty-five, married forty, and buried twenty. A bell was presented by William Thompson,* a prominent merchant of the place, and a very elegant crimson furniture for the Communion table, pulpit, and desk by Mr. Whitlock.

At a vestry meeting, 8th December, 1791, it was

"*Resolved*, That the old Church be sold, price £200. The bell, organ, and King's Coat of Arms† be removed to Trinity Church."

Until 1811 the Church had no steeple, only a belfry, with venetian blinds on the four sides.

TRINITY CHURCH.

"To be built by contract, and completed in the course of next summer: A CLOCK STORY and SPIRE upon the Tower of Trinity Church, in the City

---

* William Thompson, from 1792 to 1796, was one of the members for the County of St. John. He died at the age of 56 years, March 14th, 1802. Mrs. Thompson died at the age of 75 years, October 24th, 1824. Miss Annabella Thompson, their daughter, and the last of the family, died February 29th, 1880, aged 93 years.

"J. W. LAWRENCE, Esq.   † BOSTON, Dec. 9th, 1876.

"*My Dear Sir:* I have read your letter reciting the evidence you have collected relating to the origin of the Royal Arms in Trinity Church, Saint John, and I have not the shadow of a doubt that a little more than a hundred years ago, on the 17th of March, 1776, they left their home in the Council Chamber of the Old Town House, Boston, and sailed out of the harbour with their friends. Edward Winslow's letter to Ward Chipman, 1785, places the matter beyond any reasonable doubt.

"What place the Royal Arms occupied on the walls we cannot say; but they probably were between the portraits of King Charles II. and King James II., of more than full length, and in a splendid golden frame.

"Now that we have traced beyond a question the Royal Arms to their early home in the Council, it may be that other facts of their yet earlier history may be brought to light. . . . . .

"I am, dear Sir, your's very truly,
"EDMUND F. SLAFTER."

Rev. E. F. Slafter, of Boston, is Corresponding Secretary of the "New England Historic Genealogical Society." He married a daughter of Charles Hazen, Esq., a son of Hon. William Hazen, of Portland Parish, St. John.

F

of St. John, agreeably to a model thereof, to be seen by applying to HUGH JOHNSTON, Sen., Esquire, in the said City.

"Any person or persons desirous of undertaking the above work, will deliver, or cause to be delivered, to the said HUGH JOHNSTON proposals, in *writing*, for that purpose, on or before the 14th day of October next, to be laid before the Vestry of the said Church, under whose direction the said work is to be completed. Further particulars may be known by applying to the said HUGH JOHNSTON.

St. John, 17th August, 1809.

Mr. John Venning, while at work on the tower, 2nd of November, 1810, fell to the ground and was killed. In 1811 the Church was enlarged at the chancel end; and in 1812 the first clock in St. John placed in the tower. Until that time the bell was rung every evening at 9 o'clock; the last in that service was "Jack Cooley," receiving from the City Corporation two pounds quarterly.

On the night of the 26th of February, 1849, the cupola of the Church ignited from a spark from a fire on the north side of King Street. To save the Church the cupola had to be cut down.

The Sunday evening after, the Rector, Dr. Gray,* preached from Psalms xlviii. 9: "We have thought of Thy loving kindness, O God, in the midst of Thy Temple."

"Another building you might have had, but not the building where your fathers had worshipped; another structure, more stately perhaps, more spacious and more ornamental, but not the structure which reared its head amid the trees of the forest, and first invited the loyal sons of the infant Colony to worship within its walls. No doubt there are hearts here this evening to which these recollections are dear; yes, dearer far than the pillars and the dome and the turrets of the most splendid edifice that could have occupied the place where OLD TRINITY CHURCH has stood. As, then, your ordinances and the blessings which attend them, and your Holy House where your fathers have worshipped, are still preserved to you, lift up your hands in the Sanctuary and bless the Lord; yea, say with the Psalmist, 'We have thought of Thy loving kindness, O God, in the midst of Thy Temple.' "

*Rev. I. W. D. Gray died while on a visit to his son at Halifax, February 1, 1868, in his 70th year. For 16 years he was assistant to his father, Rev. B. G. Gray, D. D., and for 28 years Rector.

OLD TRINITY.

In 1856, Trinity Church was enlarged, with a new front, tower and steeple, and occupied the old historic ground until the fire of 1877. The Royal Arms, which passed through the perils of the Revolution, were saved, and have a place in " New Trinity," consecrated 9th of December, 1880, by the Right Rev. John Medley, D. D., Metropolitan of Canada. The preacher was the Rev. Dr. Binney, Bishop of Nova Scotia. The last Rector of "Old Trinity," and the first of "New Trinity," is the Rev. Canon Brigstocke, of Jesus College, Oxford.

ST. JOHN AND PORTLAND CHURCHES — FIRST HALF CENTURY.

Opened :		*Preacher :*
1791.	Trinity Church, ...	Rev. M. Byles, D. D.
1808.	Germain Street Methodist Church, ...	Rev. William Bennett.
1815.	St. Malachi's Chapel,*	Rev. Father Ffrench.

---

*ST. MALACHI'S CHAPEL.—In the summer of 1813, the Rev. Chas. Ffrench held the first service of the Roman Catholic Church in St. John. It was in the City Court Room, Market Square. At a meeting on the 21st of August, 1814, it was

" *Resolved,* That the thanks of the Catholics of the City of St. John be returned to the inhabitants, and to Halifax, for their liberal subscriptions

Opened.				Preacher.
1817.	St. Andrew's Kirk,	... ...	...	Rev. Geo. Burns, D. D.
1818.	Germain Street Baptist Church,†	...		Rev. Thomas Griffen.
1822.	St. George's Church, Carleton, ‡	...		Rev. Abraham Wood.
1824.	St. John Church, Wellington Row,	...		Rev. George Best.
1824.	Asylum Chapel, King Square,	...		Rev. James Priestly.
1829.	Methodist Church, Portland,	...		Rev. Richard Williams.
1829.	Grace Church, Portland,	... ...		Rev. B. G. Gray.

Until Christmas Day, 1791, the Church of England held services in the little Church, Germain Street. From that time the Methodists occupied it to Christmas Day, 1808; and from 1810 it was used by the Baptists until the opening of the Germain Street Meeting House, 1818.

JOHN WARD

was born at Peekskill, Hudson River, 1752. Sir Wm. Howe, in 1777, appointed him an Ensign in Col. Beverley Robinson's regiment. In 1778 he received a Lieutenant's commission from Sir Henry Clinton. When Major André, 1780, went to West Point in the sloop of war *Vulture* to meet Arnold, the escort was under command of Lieut. Ward. On her return to New York, Arnold, and *not* André, was on board. The latter having left

---

towards building a Catholic Church, amounting to nearly *Eight Hundred Pounds*."

And in further testimony of their gratitude, it was

Resolved, That the names of the subscribers and donations be alphabetically written on parchment, and framed, and hung in the Church, as justly entitled to the prayers of the congregation while the Church exists.

> JOHN TOOL, } Church
> BERNARD KIERNAN, } Wardens.

St. John, N. B., 21st August, 1814.

†"NEW BAPTIST MEETING HOUSE will be opened for the worship of GOD, on LORD'S DAY next, when appropriate hymns will be sung and sermons preached. Collections will be made towards the expense of building. Service at 11 a. m., and 6, evening.

"St. John, July 8th, 1818."

‡ On lots 124 and 125 Carleton, St. John's Chapel was built early after the Loyalists arrived. Occasional service was held by the Rector of Trinity, also by lay readers, the most historic was John M. Smith, *Teacher*, receiving from Trinity £20 per annum. His last service was Christmas Day, 1805. June Term, 1806, Mr. Smith was tried before Judge Upham, and ordered to hold a levee in front of City Hall, foot of King Street, in the pillory.

I am sincerly

John Ward

by land was taken prisoner. One of his captors, Paulding, married a sister of Lieut. Ward's.

The last of the troops that left New York for Parr Town were under his command. The landing was at the Lower Cove. As shelter could not be found, Lieut. Ward with the troops camped under canvas through the winter on the ground long known as the Barrack Square. The tents were trenched around and covered with spruce, brought in the boats of the transports from Partridge Island.

Lieut. Ward drew lot 412, King Street, and shortly after removed to Sussex, King's County. Ward's Creek was named after him. Returning to St. John, he entered on a successful business career.

FIRST STEAMBOAT IN NEW BRUNSWICK.

The *General Smyth*, the first steamboat in New Brunswick, was launched from the yard of John Lawton, Portland, April, 1816. Her owners were, John Ward, Hugh Johnston, Sen., Lauchlan Donaldson, J. C. F. Bremner, of St. John, and Robert Smith, Fredericton. The second steamboat, the *St. George*, 204 tons, was launched April, 1825, from the yard of Owens & Lawton, and owned by John Ward & Sons and Hugh Johnston & Co. This boat had a copper boiler, and, like the *General Smyth*, made one trip each way in the week.

The pioneer steamboat in the Bay of Fundy trade was the *St. John*. In her was placed the machinery of the *General Smyth*. In 1827 the boat was sold to James Whitney.

In 1831 the steamer *John Ward* was placed on the River, followed in 1835 by the *Fredericton*. In the latter was placed the machinery and boiler of the *St. George*. The owners of the River steamers were, John Ward & Sons and John M. Wilmot.*

* John M. Wilmot, the father of Hon. R. D. Wilmot, Lieut.-Governor of New Brunswick, for many years one of the representatives of the County of St. John. In 1833, the year of New Brunswick's Semi-Centennial, Mr. Wilmot was Mayor of the City. On retiring from business, he removed to Belmont, Sunbury County, and died, 1847, aged 72 years.

The *Royal Tar* was the first New Brunswick steamer between St. John and Boston, Thomas Reed, commander. Her principal owners were John Hammond and Daniel McLaughlin. The boat was burnt in Penobscot Bay, 20th October, 1836. On board was a caravan. Thirty-two passengers were lost.

The steam ferry boat *Victoria*, the first in the harbor, commenced running between St. John and Carleton 5th Sept., 1839.

STEAM SAW MILL.

The pioneer steam saw mill in New Brunswick was on the Straight Shore, Portland, Allan Otty and R. W. Crookshank, Jr., proprietors. It was started for the first time 29th July, 1822, in the presence of Sir James Kempt, Lieut.-Governor of Nova Scotia, and General Smyth. The first shipment of deals from St. John was to Cork, 1822, in the schooner *Amelia*, Captain Spencer, by R. Hamilton, Son & Co. *They were cut by hand.*

From 1809 to 1821 Mr. Ward was one of the members for the County of St. John.

Mr. Ward had two grand sons (Barton and Newton Wallop) living with him. On the 13th June, 1818, their uncle Charles, after returning from militia duty, left in his room two *horse pistols*. The boys, not knowing they were loaded, began playing with them; and Barton, then 10 years of age, fired one from the window at an old man, Daniel Davoust, standing on the King Street sidewalk, when he fell to the ground dead.

The father of the boys, Barton Wallop, was Naval officer at St. John, and married a daughter of Mr. Ward. She died at Newfoundland. Mr. Wallop died at his residence, Prince William Street, 27th January, 1824, in his 43rd year. He was a grandson of the 2nd Earl of Portsmouth. Barton, his son, for many years has lived in England.

On the 60th anniversary of the landing of the Loyalists, 18th May, 1843, Major Ward was presented with the following address from the officers of the artillery :

"Sir: "SAINT JOHN, May 18th, 1843.

"Assembled for the purpose of celebrating the Sixtieth Anniversary of the landing of the Loyalists in this Province, and the Fiftieth of the formation of the first (or Loyal) Company of Artillery, now embodied in the New Brunswick Regiment of Artillery, We, the Officers of that corps in St. John, gladly avail ourselves of the occasion to express the sentiments of high respect entertained towards you by our Regiment, and in which we feel assured every member of this community participates.

"Deservedly beloved and esteemed as you have ever been by all around you throughout the course of a life already extended beyond the ordinary span allotted to mortals, we claim you with pride as one of the first officers of the corps to which we have now the honor to belong; and we hail you at the same time as one of the few survivors of that gallant band, who—surrendering all save the undying honor of their sacrifice—followed the standard of their Sovereign to these shores, and whose landing we this day commemorate.

"That health and prosperity may yet long be yours, and that the evening of your days may be as free from a cloud as your past life has been unspotted, is the sincere desire of the corps in whose behalf we have the honor to subscribe ourselves,   "With great respect, Sir,

"Your obedient servants,

"T. L. NICHOLSON,	WILLIAM HUGHSON,
"Major N. B. R. A.	Captain.
"JAS. WM. BOYD,	CHARLES J. MELICK,
"Capt. and Paymaster.	Captain.
"STEPHEN K. FOSTER,	WM. WRIGHT,
Captain.	1st Lieutenant.
"EDW. B. PETERS,	N. W. WALLOP,
"Lieut. and Qr.-Master.	Lieutenant.
"CHAS. C. STEWART, 1st Lieut.	LEWIS W. DURANT, Lieut.

"To JOHN WARD, Esquire, J. P., Major, &c."

Major Ward died the 5th of August, 1846, aged 92 years. Two sons survived him: John, who died January, 1875, in his 93rd year; and Charles, January, 1882, aged 91 years.

The New-Brunswick Courier.

VOL. 1.   THURSDAY, *MAY* 2, 1811.   No. 1.

"TO THE PUBLIC.

"The subscribers have this day published the first number of a Periodical Paper, under the title of "*The New Brunswick Courier*," and solicit the patronage of the public in general.

"*The New Brunswick Courier* (for the present) will be published at Jacob S. Mott's office, Prince William Street, where subscriptions, advertisements, etc., will be thankfully received and punctually attended to.

"1. *The New Brunswick Courier* will be published every Thursday morning, on good paper and fair type, for 12s. 6d. per annum to each subscriber, payable half yearly.

"2. Subscribers living in the City, on the East side of the River, will have their paper as soon as issued from the press, and it will be forwarded to those living on the West side by the ferry boat, and to the remote parts of the Province and elsewhere with all possible dispatch.

"HENRY CHUBB & Co."

FIRST MARRIAGE NOTICE.

"Married, at Fredericton, 2nd April, 1811, by the Rev. George Pidgeon, *Rector*, Capt. ROBERT MOODIE,* of the 104th Regiment, to Miss FRANCES, third daughter of Hon. George Sproule, Surveyor General."

OBITUARY.

Died, at Fredericton, 21st December, 1811, in the 53rd year of his age, the Hon. William Balfour, Major General, and lately President and Commander-in-Chief of New Brunswick.

When Col. Carleton assumed the Government, 1784, Captain Balfour was at Fort Howe.

THE WAR OF 1812.

In the war of 1812 with the United States, privateers were fitted out to assist the vessels of war in the Bay of Fundy, and on the New England coast.

The *General Smyth*, October 1812, brought into port the American brig *Reward*, with flour, from Salem to Spain. The cargo was valued at $14,500.

The ship *Jane*, Donaldson master, from St. John to Glasgow, was captured by the ship *John*, and carried into Boston.

THE "PLUMPER."

The brig of war *Plumper*, from Halifax to St. John, was wrecked 5th December, 1812, near Dipper Harbor, in a snow storm. Her commander, Lieut. Bray, with thirty-six of the crew and seven passengers, were lost; midshipman Hall and twenty-eight of the crew were saved. On board was $70,000 of specie for the Commissariat.

---

*Capt. Moodie removed to Upper Canada, and during the rebellion of 1837 was proceeding to give information of an intended attack, and was stopped by a guard placed by William L. McKenzie four miles above Toronto. Capt. Moodie fired a pistol, on which one of the party shot him dead, the first who fell in the rebellion.

HENRY CHUBB.

His Majesty's schooner *Breem*, Lieut. Charles Hare,* July
13, 1813, brought in the American *packet*, of New York, with
flour, the *Fox*, of Portland, with flour and corn, bound for East-
port, and the *Dispatch*, from North Carolina, with flour and
naval stores.

"BY AUTHORITY.

" ALL persons now residing within the limits of the City, and its vicinity,
who consider themselves *citizens of the United States of America*, are required
forthwith to report themselves at the office of Police, held at the Recorder's
office, Prince William Street, where they will receive directions for the future
government of their conduct.

" Every stranger will, upon his arrival, immediately report himself at the
same office, and apply there for permission before his departure from the city.

"St. John, 19th June, 1813."

VOLUNTEER SEAMEN.

"Two hundred volunteer seamen having arrived to be forwarded to the
Lakes, the Commander of the Naval Force on this Station begs to solicit the
assistance of the inhabitants, who are proprietors of sleighs and sleds, in for-
warding these brave fellows on their way to Fredericton.

"St. John, 24th January, 1814. H. FLEMING SENHOUSE."

"On the 29th, at 8 a. m., the BRAVE TARS destined for Canada landed,
and, with the band of the 8th Regiment,† proceeded to Queen Square, where

---

ᶜ Married, at St. John, August 11th, 1813, by Rev. Roger Viets, Assistant
Minister, Lieut. Charles Hare, Commander of H. M. schooner *Breem*, to Miss
Mary Stewart, daughter of the late John McGeorge, Esq.

Mr. McGeorge was one of the St. John members in the first Parliament.
He was lost at sea 1795. In 1797 his widow married John Black, agent for
the British Government in the shipment of masts.

† When the war of 1812 commenced, the 104th, or King's New Brunswick
Regiment, Col. Halkett, was at Fort Howe. After leaving for Canada, the
8th Regiment took its place, succeeded by the 102nd Regiment, followed by the
98th Regiment, Col. Daniell. In 1818 the 74th Regiment, Col. French, was at
Fort Howe, the military station at St. John from 1777 to 1821. Sergeant
William Cobbett—afterwards a member of Parliament—arrived there with
a detachment of the 54th Regiment, in 1785. When only one Regiment in
the Province, a wing would be at St. John. The 74th Regiment was the last
at Fort Howe and first at the Lower Cove barracks. In 1823 the 52nd Light
Infantry, Col. Rowen, was at St. John, followed in 1827 by the 81st Regiment,
Col. Creigh. In 1830, the Rifle Brigade, Col. Eeles; 1833, the 34th Regiment, Col. Fane; 1836, 43rd Light Infantry, Col. Booth; 1838, 85th Regiment,
Col. Maxwell; 1839, 11th Regiment, Col. Goldie; 1841, 69th Regiment Col.

the sleighs were in readiness to receive them.   At 9 o'clock they set out on their journey, amid the acclamations of a large concourse of citizens."

"FOR SALE AT PUBLIC AUCTION,
"BY CROOKSHANK & JOHNSTON:

"The remaining part of the wreck of H. M. S. *Plumper*, now lying at Dipper Harbor, with guns, rigging, and unrecovered part of $70,000.   Terms at sale.   "R. EDWARDS, *Deputy Commissary General.*

"St. John, 6th July, 1815."

"HYMENEAL.—Married, at Trinity Church, July 21, 1816, by Rev. George Pidgeon, Rector, Henry Chubb, proprietor of the *New Brunswick Courier*, to Jane, daughter of the late Peter Lugrin, Esq."

CHESAPEAKE NEGROES.

A large number of slaves took refuge on board the British ships of war in the Chesapeake, and were taken to Halifax and Bermuda.   The *Romulus* arrived at St. John 25th May, 1815, with 371 from Halifax.   The negro settlement at Loch Lomond was founded by them.

In 1835, the "John Gape" letters appeared in the *Courier*, on the Crown Land Department, increasing the subscription list from 1,000 to 1,500.

In 1840, the proprietors of the *Courier* were, Henry Chubb, Samuel Seeds, and Henry J. Chubb, the latter a son of the founder.   He died at New York 26th June, 1846, aged 28 years.

In 1850 Mr. Chubb was appointed to the Mayoralty of St. John, the last by the Government.   He died 29th May, 1855, in his 69th year.

The New Brunswick Courier from the first was a commercial success, yielding only at last to changes inevitable from the introduction of the Telegraph and Ocean steam navigation.

Monins; 1842, 36th Regiment, Col. Maxwell; 1843, 30th Regiment, Col. Ormond; 1845, 33rd Regiment, Col. Whannel; 1848, 1st Royals, Col. Deane; 1850, 97th Regiment, Col. Lockyer; 1851, 72nd Regiment, Col. Murray; 1854, 76th Regiment, Col. Gardner; 1858, 62nd Regiment, Col. Daubeny; 1864, 15th Regiment, Col. Cole (succeeded by Col. Grierson); 1868, 60th Rifles, Col. Hawley; 1869, 78th Highlanders, Major Warren.   This Regiment, with the 22nd, Col. Harding, at Fredericton, were the last Regiments in New Brunswick.

TWO GRADUATES OF THE "COURIER" OFFICE.

The two first one cent newspapers in America, the *Sun* and the *Transcript*, were printed at the job office, New York, of Anderson & Smith. The third, the *Herald*, was issued from the same office, 6th May, 1835, with Bennet, Anderson & Smith, proprietors. The business manager and editor was James Gordon Bennet. Consequent on the burning of the printing office a few months later, the paper was continued by Mr. Bennet. Henry Anderson was born at St. John, and learned the printing business in the office of the *Courier*. He died at New York in his 31st year, 28th October, 1838.

ROBERT SHIVES.

In 1827 Robert Shives entered the *Courier* office, graduating in 1834. His father was a grandson of Dr. Robert Kilgour, Bishop of Aberdeen, one of the consecrators of Dr. Seabury, the first Bishop in the United States.

MARRIED, at Parish of Portland, Sunday evening, 14th, July, 1811, by Rev. Oliver Arnold, Rector of Sussex, Mr. Robert Shives, Merchant, of St. John, to Martha, daughter of Mr. John Wiggins, of said Parish.

G

While on a visit to Scotland, their son Robert was born. Mr. Shives died at St. John 30th December, 1824, aged 37 years.

In 1866, Robert Shives was appointed Emigrant Agent for New Brunswick, and retired from the Press. He died at the age of 64 years, 7th January, 1879.

THE NEW BRUNSWICK NEWSPAPERS THE FIRST HALF CENTURY.

First Issue.		Publisher.
1783.	The Royal Gazette and Nova Scotia Intelligencer, ...	Lewis & Ryan.
1784.	The Royal New Brunsw'k Gazette & Gen. Advertiser,	" "
1785.	The Royal Gazette and Weekly Advertiser, ...	Christopher Sower. born 1756; died 1799.
1785.	The St. John Gazette and General Advertiser,	... John Ryan. born 1761; died 1847.
1799.	The St. John Gazette and Weekly Advertiser,	... Jacob S. Mott. born 1773; died 1814.
1799.	The Royal Gazette and New Brunswick Advertiser,	John Ryan. born 1761; died 1847.
1804.	The New Brunswick Chronicle, ...	Michael Ryan. born 1784; died 1829.
1806.	The Fredericton Telegraph, ...	Michael Ryan. born 1784; died 1829.
1807.	The Royal Gazette and New Brunswick Advertiser,	Jacob S. Mott. born 1773; died 1814.
1808.	The Times and True Briton, ...	Wm. Durant & Co. born 1780; died 1832.
1811.	The New Brunswick Courier, ...	Henry Chubb & Co. born 1787; died 1855.
1811.	The City Gazette, ...	Wm. Durant & Co. born 1780; died 1832.
1815.	The Gazette and New Brunswick Advertiser, ...	Ann Mott. born 1774; died 1861.
1815.	The New Brunswick Royal Gazette, Fredericton,	*George F. Lugrin. born 1791; died 1835.
1819.	The Star and Commercial Intelligencer, ...	Reynolds & Younghusband. born 1787; died 1853; born 1798; died 1850.
1819.	The St. Andrew's Herald,†	John M. Cochren.
1825.	The Miramichi Mercury (changed to Gleaner), ...	James A. Pierce. born 1804; died 1865.

* In 1822 Mr. Lugrin retired from the Press, and was succeeded in the office of King's Printer by John Simpson, who died 1863, in his 64th year.

† The St. Andrew's Herald, was the property of a Company. Its editor, John Cochren, early retired, and was succeeded by David Howe, brother of Hon. Joseph Howe. In 1822, Peter Stubbs, a merchant of St. Andrews, purchased the Herald; his foreman was John H. Story. In 1831 he sold it to his son John; the paper shortly after was discontinued. From 1820 to 1827, Mr. Stubbs was one of the members for Charlotte. In 1832 he returned to Scotland, and died 1840, in his 57th year.

First Issue.		Publisher.
1827.	*The British Colonist*, ...	John Hooper. born 1791; died 1869.
1828.	*The Weekly Observer*, ...	Cameron & Seeds. born 1799; died 1858; born 1806; died 1864.
1830.	*The St. Andrew's Courant*, ...	Colin Campbell. born 1783; died 1843.
1833.	*The Fredericton Watchman*, ...	George F. Lugrin. born 1791; died 1835.
1833.	*The St. Andrew's Standard*,	George N. Smith. born 1789; died 1854.

The Commercial News and General Advertiser, the first tri-weekly penny newspaper in the British Colonies, was issued at St. John September 16, 1839, by George E. Fenety, now Queen's Printer.

THE FIRST NEW BRUNSWICK TELEGRAM.

"ST. JOHN, 30th April, 1851.

"By Telegraph from St. Andrews.

" TO DR. WILLIAM BAYARD.

" Being the first subscriber to the Electric Telegraph Company, I am honored by the first communication to your city announcing this great and wonderful work God has made known to man by giving us control of His lightnings. "Signed. JOHN WILSON."

GOVERNORS AND ADMINISTRATORS OF NEW BRUNSWICK.

Born.	Appointed.	Title.			Died.
1736	1784	Thomas Carleton, Gov.-General B. N. A., ...		.....	1817
1736	1786	Thomas Carleton, Lieut.-Governor,	......	......	1817
1736	1803	Hon. Gabriel G. Ludlow, Administrator, ...		......	1808
1745	1808	Hon. Edward Winslow, "	......	......	1815
1758	1808	Gen. Martin Hunter, "	......	......	1847
......	1808	Lieut.-Col. G. Johnston, "	......	......	......
1758	1809	Gen. Martin Hunter, "	......	......	1847
1758	1811	Gen. William Balfour, "	......	......	1811
1758	1811	Gen. Martin Hunter, "	......	......	1847
1767	1812	Gen. G. Stracy Smyth, "	......	......	1823
1760	1813	Gen. Sir Thomas Saumarez, "	......	.....	1858
1767	1814	Gen. G. Stracy Smyth, "	......	......	1823
1752	1816	Lieut.-Col. Wm. Harris Hailes, "	......	......	1819
1767	1817	Gen. G. Stracy Smyth, Lieut.-Governor, ...		......	1823
1754	1823	Hon. Ward Chipman, Administrator,	......	......	1824
1771	1824	Hon. John Murray Bliss, "	......	......	1834
1777	1824	Sir Howard Douglas, Lieut.-Governor,	......	......	1861
1770	1829	Hon. William Black, Administrator,	......	......	1866
.....	1831	Sir Archibald Campbell, Lieut.-Governor,		.. ...	1843
1778	1837	Sir John Harvey, "	......	......	1852
1787	1841	Col. Sir Wm. M. G. Colebrooke, "	......	......	1870

Born.	Appointed.	Title.			Died.
1805	1848	Sir Edmund W. Head, Lieut. Governor,	.....	......	1868
1814	1854	Hon. H. T. Manners Sutton, "	......	......	1877
1829	1861	Hon. Sir Arthur Gordon, "	......	......	
1805	1866	Sir C. Hastings Doyle, Administrator,	......	......	1883
1805	1867	Sir C. Hastings Doyle, Lieut.-Governor,	......	......	1883
......	1867	Lieut.-Col. F. Pym Harding, "	......	......	
1809	1868	Hon. L. Allan Wilmot, "	......	......	1878
1818	1873	Hon. Samuel Leonard Tilley, "	......	......	
1798	1878	Hon. Edward B. Chandler, "	......	......	1880
1809	1880	Hon. Robert Duncan Wilmot, "	......	......	

CHIEF JUSTICES OF NEW BRUNSWICK.

George Duncan Ludlow was born at Long Island, New York, 1734. In early life he was an apothecary, but left it for the law. In 1769 Governor Colden appointed him to the Council, with a seat on the Bench. On the death of the Chief Justice of New York, 1778, Governor Elliott appointed William Smith. To conciliate Judge Ludlow, he gave him the Master of Rolls, £300 salary, with fees, also the office of Superintendent of Police, with 365 guineas salary and perquisites. At the close of the war Judge Ludlow, with his brother Gabriel (the first Mayor of St. John), went to England, and was appointed Chief Justice of New Brunswick, with a salary of £500 sterling. On their arrival at St. John they were joined by their families from New York. The wife of the Chief Justice was a daughter of George Duncan, whose house took fire in 1757, at a time Mrs. Duncan with eight of their children were in the third story. Before the fire was discovered, the stairs were in flames and escape cut off. As the ladders were not long enough, beds were placed on the ground, and Mrs. Duncan entreated to throw the children out and jump herself. Frances, the eldest, in her 20th year, only escaped. A year later she was married to Mr. Ludlow, and her father resided with them to his death. The Chief Justice obtained a grant on the River St. John, above Fredericton, and named it Spring Hill, after the residence of Governor Colden. He had one son and two daughters; the eldest married Richard Harrison, a Councillor of New York; the other, John Robinson, afterwards Mayor of St. John and Province Treasurer. The son was a member of the firm of Ludlow, Frazer & Robinson, Fredericton. After the death of his father, he returned to New York. The Chief Justice died November 13, 1808, in his 75th year. Mrs. Ludlow died at the residence of her son-in-law, St. John, 1824, in her 88th year. Dr. E. G. Ludlow, a grandson of the Chief Justice, died recently at New York in his 83rd year, the last in the male line of New Brunswick's first Chief Justice.

Born.	Appointed.						Died.
1734	1784	George Duncan Ludlow,	.. ...	......	......		1808
1740	1809	Jonathan Bliss,	......	......	......	......	1822
1754	1822	John Saunders,	......	.....	.....	......	1834
1787	1834	Ward Chipman,	......	......	......	......	1851
1805	1851	James Carter,	......	......	......	......	1878

Born.	Appointed.						Died.
1796	1865	Robert Parker,	......	......	......	......	1865
1813	1865	William Johnston Ritchie,*		......	......	......	
1817	1875	John Campbell Allen, ...		......	......	......	

Born.	Appointed.	ASSISTANT JUDGES.					Died.
1725	1784	James Putnam,	......	......	.....	.. ...	1789
1741	1784	Isaac Allen, ...	......	......	.....	.....	1806
1747	1784	Joshua Upham,	......	......	... ..	.....	1808
1754	1790	John Saunders, *vice* Putnam,		......	......	......	1834
1746	1807	Edward Winslow, *vice* Allen,		......	......	......	1815
1754	1809	Ward Chipman, *vice* Upham,		......	.....	......	1824
1771	1816	John Murray Bliss, *vice* Winslow,			......	......	1834
1788	1822	Edward J. Jarvis, *vice* Saunders,			......	......	1852
1773	1823	William Botsford, *vice* Jarvis,		......	......	......	1864
1787	1825	Ward Chipman, *vice* Chipman, ...			......	......	1851
1805	1834	James Carter, *vice* Chipman,		......	......	......	1878
1796	1834	Robert Parker, *vice* Bliss,		......	......	......	1865
1796	1845	George Frederick Street, *vice* Botsford,			......	......	1855
1809	1851	Lemuel Allan Wilmot, *vice* Carter,			......	......	1878
1798	1854	Neville Parker,† (additional Judge),			......	.....	1869
1813	1855	William Johnston Ritchie, *vice* Street,			.....	......	
1817	1865	John Campbell Allen, *vice* Parker,			......	.....	
1805	1865	John Wesley Weldon, *vice* Ritchie,			......	......	
1808	1868	Charles Fisher, *vice* Wilmot,		......	......	......	1880
1820	1870	A. Rainsford Wetmore, *vice* N. Parker,			......	......	
1817	1875	Charles Duff, *vice* Allen,		......	......	......	1882
1820	1879	Acalus L. Palmer, (additional Judge),			....	......	
1839	1880	George King, *vice* Fisher,		......	......	......	
1829	1882	John J. Fraser, *vice* Duff,		......	......	......	

JUDGES COURT OF VICE-ADMIRALTY.

Appointed.		Appointed.	
1787	Gabriel G. Ludlow.	1833	Neville Parker.
1803	William Botsford.	1838	Wm. B. Kinnear.
1808	Charles J. Peters.	1846	Robert L. Hazen.
1828	Robert Parker.	1875	Charles Watters.

PROVINCIAL SECRETARIES.

App'd.		App'd.		App'd.	
1784	Jonathan Odell.	1856	R. D. Wilmot.	1871	G. L. Hatheway.
1812	Wm. F. Odell.	1857	S. L. Tilley.	1872	John J. Fraser.

*Chief Justice Supreme Court of Canada.

† In 1838 the Master of Rolls was created, Neville Parker, Master. In 1852 it was abolished, and Mr. Parker made Judge, with rank next Chief Justice.

App'd.		App'd.		App'd.	
1844	Alfred Reade.	1865	A. H. Gillmor.	1878	Wm. Wedderburn.
1845	John S. Saunders.	1866	S. L. Tilley.	1882	Pierre Landry.
1848	John R. Partelow.	1867	J. A. Beckwith.	1883	William Elder.
1854	S. L. Tilley.				

ATTORNEYS GENERAL.

App'd.		App'd.		App'd.	
1784	Ward Chipman.	1854	Charles Fisher.	1866	Charles Fisher.
1785	Jonathan Bliss.	1856	John H. Gray.	1867	A. R. Wetmore.
1809	Thos. Wetmore.	1857	Charles Fisher.	1870	George King.
1828	Robert Parker.	1861	Albert J. Smith.	1878	John J. Fraser.
1828	Charles J. Peters.	1862	John M. Johnston.	1882	Ezek'l McLeod.
1848	L. A. Wilmot.	1865	John C. Allen.	1883	And'w G. Blair.
1851	John A. Street.	1865	Albert J. Smith.		

SOLICITORS GENERAL.*

App'd.		App'd.		App'd.	
1784	Ward Chipman.	1834	George F. Street.	1866	Edw'd Williston.
1809	John M. Bliss.	1846	Wm. B. Kinnear.	1867	Chas N. Skinner.
1816	William Botsford.	1854	J. M. Johnston.	1879	J. H. Crawford.
1823	Ward Chipman, Jun.	1856	John C. Allen.	1882	F. E. Morton.
1825	Charles J. Peters.	1857	Charles Watters.	1883	Rob't J. Ritchie.
1828	Robert Parker.				

ADVOCATES GENERAL.

App'd.		App'd.		App'd.	
1887	Ward Chipman.	1825	George F. Street.	1846	Wm. Wright.
1809	Ward Chipman, Jun.	1834	John Simcoe Saunders.	1865	Wm. Jack.

CLERKS OF THE CROWN IN THE SUPREME COURT.

App'd.		App'd.		App'd.	
1785	Colin Campbell.	1822	Wm. H. Minchin.	1851	Andrew Barbarie.
1796	Thos. Wetmore.	1825	Charles S. Putnam.	1858	A. R. Wetmore.
1804	William F. Odell.	1837	George F. Berton.	1865	Charles Watters.
1819	Henry Bliss.	1843	John A. Street.	1867	W. H. Tuck.

MAYORS OF SAINT JOHN.

Born.	Appointed.						Died.
1736	1785	Gabriel G. Ludlow,	......	......	......	......	1808
1742	1795	William Campbell,	......	......	......	......	1823
1762	1816	John Robinson,	......	......	......	......	1828
1770	1828	William Black,	......	......	......	......	1866
1786	1829	Lauchlan Donaldson,	......	......	......	......	1873

*The Solicitor General's office was not filled in 1865. From 1869 to 1879 it was abolished.

Born.	Appointed.							Died.
1770	1832	William Black,	......	......	......	......		1866
1775	1833	John M. Wilmot,	......	......	......	......		1847
1789	1834	Benjamin L. Peters,	......	......	......	......		1852
1798	1835	William H. Street,	......	......	......	......		1876
1799	1836	John Robertson,	.. ...	......	......	......		1876
1803	1837	Robert F. Hazen,	......	......	......	......		1874
1770	1840	William Black,	......	......	......	......		1866
1786	1843	Lauchlan Donaldson,	......	......	......	......		1873
1796	1847	John R. Partelow,	......	......	......	......		1865
1798	1847	William H. Street,	......	......	......	......		1876
1809	1849	Robert Duncan Wilmot,		......	......	......		
1787	1850	Henry Chubb,	......	.....	......	......		1855

ELECTED BY COMMON COUNCIL.

Born.	Elected.		Died.	Born.	Elected.	
1786	1851	Thomas Harding,	1854	1816	1853	James Olive.
1804	1852	William O. Smith,	1871			

ELECTED BY CITIZENS.

Born.	Elected.		Died.	Born.	Elected.	
1816	1854	James Olive.		1827	1870	Thomas M. Reed.
1804	1855	Wm. O. Smith,	1871	1839	1874	A. Chip. Smith.
1811	1859	Thomas McAvity.		1822	1877	Sylvester Z. Earle.
1795	1863	Isaac Woodward,	1879	1829	1879	Charles R. Ray.
1831	1866	Aaron Alward.		1831	1881	Simeon Jones.

WARD CHIPMAN.

Ward Chipman was a Massachusetts Loyalist,* and through the war Deputy Muster-Master General at New York, receiving from its close to his death a pension of £96 sterling. In addition to the offices held under the Crown in New Brunswick, in 1796 he was appointed by the British Government Agent before the Commission to determine the St. Croix of the Treaty of 1783. On this he was over two years, with a salary of £940 sterling per annum. In 1816, under the Treaty of Ghent, he was agent

*The father of Ward Chipman was a member of the Massachusetts Bar. He died 1768, in his 47th year, leaving a widow, two sons, and four daughters. One married John Gray, the eminent shipowner of Salem, grandfather of Judge Gray of the Supreme Court of the United States. Of the family, Ward alone adhered to the Crown.

for the Crown to locate the N. W. angle of Nova Scotia.   This he held to his death, with the salary of the former agency.

At the close of the American war, the Company in London for the Education of the Heathen natives and their children in English families in some trade, mystery or lawful calling, changed its field of operation from New England to New Brunswick, with its Indian College at Sussex.   For many years its teacher was Joseph R. Leggitt, receiving from the Company £30 per annum.   The missionary to the Indians was the Rev. Oliver Arnold, with a salary of £50 currency.   Mr. Arnold often had four Indian youths in his family, receiving for each £20, and what service they could give out of school hours.   The disburse-ments of the Company in 1823, the last year of Ward Chipman's Secretary-Treasurship, were £770; of this he received as salary £50 sterling, and Hon. John Coffin,* a half-pay Lieut.-General in the British army, £125 sterling as Superintendent.   Ward Chipman, 1786, married a daughter of Hon. Wm. Hazen, and died at Fredericton, 1824, in his 70th year, while Administrator of the Government.   Mrs. Chipman died at St. John in her 87th year, 18th of May, 1852, the 69th anniversary of the *landing of the Loyalists.*

Ward Chipman, Jun., (1824) one of the members for the County of St. John, and Speaker of the House, succeeded, on his father's death, to his seat on the Bench and in the Council, as well as to the more lucrative position of Agent for the Crown in determining the N. W. angle of Nova Scotia.   He also suc-ceeded his father as Secretary-Treasurer, holding the office to the close (1834) of the Company's philanthropic work in behalf of the Indians in New Brunswick.   In 1825 Ward Chipman was appointed by the British Government (and again in 1833) Umpire to apportion the customs duties between Upper and Lower Canada, receiving for each service £700.   His duties in connection with the N. W. angle of Nova Scotia, with its salary of £940 sterling, terminated in his mission, in 1829, to the

---

* Hon. John Coffin was present at the battle of Bunker Hill.   He died at the Coffin Manor, Nerepis, K. C., 12th May, 1838, aged 87 years.

Hague. In 1817, Ward Chipman married a daughter of Henry Wright, Collector of Customs at St. John, and died at the age of 64 years, 1851. Mrs. Chipman, the *last of the family*, died, aged 83 years, the 4th of July, 1876, the 100th anniversary of AMERICAN INDEPENDENCE.

RECORDERS OF SAINT JOHN.

Born.	Appointed.						Died.
1754	1785	Ward Chipman,*	......	......	......	......	1824
1768	1809	Thomas Wetmore,	......	......	......	......	1828
1773	1810	William Botsford,	......	......	......	......	1864
1787	1815	Ward Chipman, Jun.,		......	......	......	1851
1788	1822	Edward J. Jarvis,	......	......	......	......	1852
1796	1824	Robert Parker,	......	......	......	......	1865
1796	1830	William B. Kinnear,	......	......	......	......	1868
1803	1835	Robert F. Hazen,	......	......	......	......	1874
1796	1836	William B. Kinnear,	......	......	......	......	1868
1808	1846	Robert L. Hazen,	......	......	......	......	1874
1831	1874	William H. Tuck.	......	......	......	......	

CHAMBERLAINS OF SAINT JOHN.

Born.	App'd.		Died.	Born.	App'd.		Died.
1742	1785	George Leonard,	1826	1796	1827	John R. Partelow,	1865
1748	1787	Isaac Bell,	1805	1792	1843	Thomas Merritt,	1869
1754	1793	James Codner,	1821	1820	1861	James R. Ruel.	
1755	1801	John Thomson,	1825	1833	1870	William Sandall,	1880
1758	1818	Thomas Sancton,	1830	1845	1880	Frederick Sandall.	

"* ABACA, NEW PROVIDENCE, 12th Sept., 1787.

"MY DEAR CHIPMAN,—

"We are safe and well, after nearly a month's passage. I have every prospect of doing well in this country. Two gentlemen who divided the business at the Bar between them have retired upon their estates. The Attorney General is as lazy a fellow as your's, and is going very fast to the other world. . . . . . . May you, my dear Chipman, enjoy every blessing your imagination can figure. I have no doubt but in a few years you will receive £400 or £500 from your Government. I think your income must increase. Long, my dear fellow, may you be at the head of your profession. . . . .

"No turtles of any size are at present to be got, but are brought every day into Nassau, and I have given orders for two very handsome fellows to be put on board the vessel which touches there, for you. I hope they will be delivered to you in high health, and well loaded with green fat and other nice bits, sufficient for a *Recorder's* feast to his CORPORATION.

"WILLIAM WYLLY."

COMMON CLERKS OF SAINT JOHN.

Born.	App'd.		Died.	Born.	App'd.		Died.
1721	1785	Bartholomew Crannell,	1790	1809	1847	Jas. Wm. Boyd,	1859
1746	1790	Elias Hardy,	1799	1811	1849	Geo. Wheeler,	1855
1772	1799	Chas. Jeffrey Peters,	1848	1818	1855	W. R. M. Burtis,	1882
1800	1823	James Peters, Jun.,	1847	1827	1863	B. Lester Peters.	

SHERIFFS OF SAINT JOHN.

App'd.		Died.	App'd.		Died.
1785	William Sanford Oliver,	1813	1816	James White,	1858
1792	John Holland,	1806	1847	Charles Johnston,	1858
1797	William Sanford Oliver,	1813	1858	James A. Harding.	
1813	William Hazen,	1816			

FIRST GOVERNMENT HOUSE.

The first Government House, Fredericton, was built in 1787, and burnt in the fire of 1825. In 1816 it was purchased by the Province from Governor Carleton, with 50 acres on the River St. John, for £3,650. A view of this old historic building will be a fitting close to

Foot-Prints;

OR,

NEW BRUNSWICK'S CENTENNIAL SOUVENIR.

Grantees Parr Town,

1783.

Allen, William 13	Bean, Thomas 90	Bowland, Nicholas 834
Allen, Isaac 56 57	Bennison, George 109	Bostick, Daniel 845
Allen, Benjamin 377	Blair, David 122	Birmingham, James 833
Anderson, Benjamin 74	Bunce, Joseph 129	Brundage, James 850
Anderson, Wm. 164 1343	Bentley, John 130	Brundage, Nathan 650
Anderson, Henry 1351	Beardsley, John 151	Brundage, Daniel 856
Anderson, Peter 973	Bedell, Stephen	Barton, Edward 899
Anderson, Joseph 1027	Bell, Isaac	Barry, Thomas 902
Arnold, Oliver 95	Botsford, Amos 202	Beck, Joseph 903
Andrew, George 128	Barclay, Thos. 203 204	Black, James 909
Alward, Joseph 188 1408	Beatie, John 207	Barckley, James 962
Alwood, Oswald 306	Blair, George 239	Barckley, Abraham 963
Alwood, Joseph 343	Bruce, David 244	Barkly, William 964
Alwood, Silas 573	Brown, John 311	Baxter, Stephen 968
Alstine, Lewis 320	Brown, Hugh 322	Brundage, Andrew 969
Alstine, Joseph 781	Butler, Thomas 323	Branscomb, Arthur 975
Alstine, David 1007	Butler, James 326	Brundage, Joshua 977
Albright, John 381	Brush, Samuel & R. 333	Bogle, William 987
Ashford, William 436	Bogart, Isaac 337	Buston, Thomas 1005
Appleby, Benjamin 688	Bedell, William 338	Barlow, Thomas 1015
Atkinson, William 196	Beardsley, Paul 374	Bookhout, John 1028
Adams, John 703	Bucklaw, Sarah 388	Britton, William 1050
Allison, William 763	Barry, Lewis 444	Burton, James 1051
Alger, John 901	Barker, John 464	Britton, Joseph 1052
Alger, Alexander 914	Bemon, William 478	Bailes, Edward 1054
Alger, James 919	Boyne, Alexander 483	Bampton, Paul 1074
Aymer, Francis 1125	Blanchvill, Patrick 501	Balentine, Alex. 1097
Aerig, Rachael 1137	Bellman, William 506	Bowen, Ansell 1109
Atwood, Isaac 1177	Burtis, William 578	Bourdett, O. 1118 1237
Allan, Anthony 1192	Banker, Abraham 581	Buckley, Thomas 1122
Atthouse, John 1288	Bowen, William 588	Brawn, Charles 1142
Aston, Samuel 1295	Baily, Oliver 593	Barnes, Thomas 1152
Armour, May 1323	Barns, John 609	Branson, Ely 1169
Arnold, Amasa 66	Baily, Joseph 648	Barbarie, John 1191
Arrowsmith, Wm. 1326	Bonsall, Rich'd 672 1413	Barbarie, Olliver 1193
Adair, Robert 1350	Burnington, James 695	Butler, Michael 1213
Angus, Robert, 1414	Bowen, Francis 726	Barker, Abijah 1260
Arnold, Oliver, water lot	Brown, Adam 727	Bawn, Samuel 1263
Barker, Thomas 2	Burns, William 765	Brawnall, Joshua 1267
Bedell, John 7	Burns, Samuel 768	Bremerton, George 1271
Bedell, Joseph 8 33	Blakeny, David 770	Bremerton, James 1273
Bell, Jacob 19	Blakeny, William 777	Brinkerhoff, Abr. 1279
Bedell, Paul 32	Baxter, George 789	Boggs, John 1304
Brownrigg, John 42 43	Branner, Ezekiel 794	Bostick, Isaac 1313
Bridgeham, Ebenezer 46	Burden, Thomas 816	Brawn, Bostwick 1319

(1)

Bosworth, Thomas	1324	
Brawn, Daniel	1328	
Bryanth, Seth	1335	
Bell, James	1349	
Butler, Josiah	1356	
Bayle, Richard	1358	
Barton, Michael	1359	
Blair, James	1363	
Brigs, John	1389	
Blades, Christop'r	1396	
Bourns, John	1406	
Beveridge, David	1415	
Boyne, James	1422	
Burns, Samuel	1438	
Butler, Peter	1439	
Bell, John	1442	
Baxter, Stevens	1446	
Britt, James	1455	
Burgis, John	1459	
Brown, Mary	1256	
Clowes, Ger. 9 120	407	
Clowes, Timothy	53	
Clowes, Samuel	85	
Clowes, John	139	
Colvill, John	50 159	
Camp, John	16 499	
Camp, Abia'r, jr.	95 192	
Camp, Abia'r, sr.	20 69	
Camp, Eldad	641	
Camp, John, jr.	935	
Campbell, Collin	18 61	
Campbell, Walter	177	
Campbell, Dugald	426	
Campbell, Mary	707	
Campbell, Robert	708	
Campbell, Robert, jr.	709	
Campbell, William	723	
Campbell, Laughlan	991	
Campbell, Donald	1215	
Codner, James	48	
Challoner, Walter	58	
Connor, Constant	64	
Connor, John	1011	
Carman, Richard	82	
Crannell, Barth.	88	
Crannell, Francis	428	
Crannell, Mary	431	
Cluet, John	105	
Coffin, John Major	112	
Coffin, Guy Carleton	141	
Cockran, John	113	
Cockran, William	916	
Clapper, Garret	114	
Clayton, Samuel	124	
Chase, Lydia	171	
Chase, William	386	
Chase, Shadrack	568	
Cullen, Isaac	219	
Currie, Ross	225	
Currie, Joshua	655	
Currie, David	653	
Curry, Richard	652	
Curry, John	1217	
Christal, John	227	
Cameron, James	247	
Cameron, Duncan	927	
Cameron, Daniel	1272	
Cole, Stephen	292	
Cole, William	767	
Cole, Richard	918	
Cole, David	1185	
Coalle, Ishmael	441	
Craddock, Thomas	297	
Clarke, Joseph	313	
Clarke, Nehemiah	314	
Clarke, Samuel	784	
Clarke, Thomas	1113	
Clarke, John	947 1115	
do.,	1140 1334	
Clarke, Alexander	1232	
Clarke, James 1255	1340	
Clarke, James, jr.	1339	
Christopher, Rachael	376	
Cable, David	382	
Cable, Jabez	1315	
Cable, Denbo	1342	
Combs, Dennis	410	
Combs, Samuel	650	
Coomby,	852	
Carrington, James	413	
Colling, Thomas	414	
Cummings, Allen	727	
Cummins, Daniel	1278	
Crab, James	465	
Crab, John	565	
Crab, Stephen	646	
Crab, John, jr.	647	
Chesser, Thomas	481	
Corneilanson, John	493	
Carre, Henry	505	
Carre, William	711	
Carey, Thomas	1376	
Carns, Robert	697	
Cooke, Jordan	511	
Cook, Charles	1014	
Cook, Robert	1318	
Cook, John	1398	
Cook, Jacob	1441	
Cudney, Ezekiel	543	
Close, David	624	
Castin, Benjamin	714	
Castin, Isaiah	715	
Castin, Thomas	830	
Clinton, William	719	
Curtis, Andrew	721	
Clews, Jonathan	730	
Cantwell, Richard	758	
Christy, Shadrack	771	
Christie, James	922	
Crissie, Matthias	875	
Cypher, Lodwick	787	
Conce, Joseph	799	
Cleveland, Katura	805	
Cleveland, William	1312	
Carlisle, Robert	809	
Cunningham, Myles	811	
Carl, Jonas	827	
Cornwall, William	847	
Cornwall, Andrew	1230	
Crawford, Thomas	848	
Crawford, Jno. 1012	1259	
Crawford, Wm. sr.	1316	
Crawford, Wm. jr.	1317	
Costilla, Francis	884	
Connelly, John	895	
Connelly, Dennis	1064	
Carr, Laurence	896	
Card, Elijah	1021	
Culvar, Jonas, jr.	957	
Culvar, Jonas, sr.	958	
Craig, James	983	
Craig, Robert	1094	
Canby, Joseph	1006	
Cunard, Robert	1008	
Clements, Peter	1055	
Crandy, John	1076	
Compton, William	1104	
Chubb, John	1151	
Cotter, Michael	1159	
Carpenter, Thomas	1165	
Coffield, Thomas	1167	
Carver, Caleb	1209	
Case, Elisha	1250	
Case, John	1458	
Charles, Claudius	1303	
Callahan, Nicholas	1327	
Conklin, Samuel	1344	
Chittish, Robert	1424	
Cuthbert, James	1429	
Dibble, Polly	17	
Dibble, Fyler heirs	60	
Dibble, Walter	116	
Dibble, Frederic	117	
DePeyster, Ab'm 21	103	
DePeyster, Frederic	84	
Dunbar, George	49	
Dunbar, Elizabeth	1355	
Dickinson, Turtulus	78	
Dickinson, Sam'l 96	398	
Dickinson, Isaac	814	
Dickinson, James	164	

Name	No.	Name	No.	Name	No.
Hallet, Joseph	212	Hall, John	1390	Johnston, William	1063
Hallet, Moses	232	Hutchison, Fos'r 439	440	Johnston, Cornel's	1066
Harding, Wm.	5 35	Hughes, Samuel	800	Joslin, Andrew	372
Hawser, Fred'ck	6 34	Hughes, John	905	Jewel, Ezekiel	521
Hewlit, Richard	12 55	Holdridge, David	796	Jewel, Abraham	530
Harrison, James	14	Helmick, Frederick	560	Jordan, Francis	967
Harrison, Charles	91	Hume, Ely	951	Jordan, John	1031
Harrison, John	508	Hamilton, John	613	Jordan, Thomas	1032
Handford, Thomas	186	Hamilton, Gorham	1391	Jennings, Thomas	997
Hingston, William	62	Haviland, Auchimas	653	Judson, Chapman	1114
Hustace, Stephen	75	Haviland, Isaac	1155	Jenkins, John	1341
Hustace, James	636	Hoyt, Joseph	24	Jones, Hugh	943
Hustace, John	1172	Henley, James	217	Knutton, John	44
Hustace, Lewis	1262	Horsie, Samuel	803	Knutton, William	45
Hubbard, William	165	Harvey, John	818	Knutton, Joseph	562
Howe, Caleb	195	Hardenbrook, Able	1098	Kennedy, Patrick	83
Hatch, Christopher	81	Hays, William	1382	Kennedy, John	1068
Hatch, Haws	157	Hitchcock, John	619	Kennedy, John, jr	1069
Horton, Nathan	120	Hagamon, John	1449	Kennedy, William	1070
Horsfield, Thomas	92	Hacket, Mary Ann	1257	Kennedy, David	1353
Harris, George	131	Howland, Elenor	563	Ketchum, James	94
Horsfield, James	110	Hataby, Richard	690	Kautzman, Cath. 97	561
Harris, William	823	Horsely,	693	Kerr, James	142
Harris, Joseph	824	Hardcastle, Joseph	651	Knight, Benjamin	182
Harris, Thomas	966	Harmond, Burney	716	Kean, William	231
Heller, Elizabeth	137	Higgins, Abraham	791	Kain, Hugh	371
Huggerford, Wm.	147	Homes, Absalom	1211	Kelly, William,	236
Huggerford, P., jr.	149	Higby, George	1188	Kent, Stephen	307
Huggerford, P., sr.	150	Higby, Jonas	1281	Kent, Rachael	325
Halland, Richard	197	Heslop, John	392	Kursto, Conrad	364
Halland, Jesse	1059	Hayton, William	970	Kenny, William	487
Hatfield, David	1160	Hull, Sylvester	1022	Kahee, Edward	488
Hatfield, Daniel	1161	Haid, Jonathan	1003	Kay, George	626
Hatfield, Abraham	1163	Hampton, Abner	1065	Keef, Daniel	766
Hatfield, Isaac	1164	Heydecker, George	1075	Keef, James	1013
Hunt, Samuel	586	Hargile, Christop'r	1106	Kingston, Dorothea	844
Hunt, Casby	949	Harned, Nathaniel	1128	Kingston, James	1058
Hunt, John	1321	Hendricks, Conrad	1134	Kirk, John	1234
Harden, Mary	336	Herster, Andrew	1148	Kelly, John,	625
Hadon, James	935	Hammel, John	1150	Leonard, Thomas	1
Heddon, Zoph 1388	1437	Ingham, Isaac	296	Leonard, George, jr.	38
Humphrey, Wm.	208	Innis, James	399	Leonard, George	39
Hartshorn, Davidson	291	Ives, David	994	Lester, Benjamin	50
Hawly, William	315	Ingles, Alexander	1222	Lester, Benjamin, sr.	93
Halsy, Elisha	1258	Jones, Caleb 3	211	Lester, Mordecai	415
Helsy, John	849	Jones, Nahaum 28	77	Lester, Thomas	111
Herson, Benjamin	877	Jones, Simon	76	Lester, Jacob	415
Hazen, Joseph	569	Jones, John 906	1380	Lester, Sarah	904
Hina, Christopher	369	do.	1457	Lester, Mary	1287
Hamblin, William	370	Jones, Samuel	1168	Lewis, William	59
Hicks, Robert 396	912	Jarvis, Samuel	86	Lyon, John	73
Hicks, John	462	Jarvis, Munson	87	Lyon, Hezekiah	1337
Holt, Moses	228	Jarvis, Nathaniel	910	Lawton, Isaac	89
Holder, Jacob	566	Jackson, Basil	206	Lawton, Mary	435
Holder, John	572	Jackson, Robert	937	Lawton, Thomas	512
Henry, George	1394	Johnston, Nathaniel	321	Lawton, James	1247
Henry, James	1421	Johnston, Robert	936	Love, James	218

H

Wray, John	433	Waters, Abraham	585	Wagstaff, Thos. H.	984
Webster, Elizabeth	503	Waters, Abijah	832	Wheeler, George	988
Whitney, Sylvanus	387	Waters, Daniel	854	Wheeler, Rynard	989
Whitney, Nathan, jr.	666	Wheaton, James	775	Waddington, Bor's	1040
Whitney, Nathan	675	Watty, Philip	928	Worden, Jarvis	1072
Wick, Zapher	528	White, Henry	220	Worden, Jeremiah	1270
Woodley, George	575	White, Peter	238	Warner, Christop'r	1120
Webb, Sarah	645	White, Thos. 385	956	Warner, James	1223
Webb, William	1206	White, Andrew	559	Warner, John 1302	1428
Wooley, Elihu	683	White, Wm. 570	655	Watt, John	1197
Whaley, Thomas	684	White, Vincent	954	Young, Thomas	221
Whoathin, Morris	689	White, John 1010	1182	Young, George	637
Ward, John	412	do.	1240	Young, Francis	1124
Ward, Daniel	1162	White, Peleg	1331	Younghusband, G.	1117
Ward, Usal	1364	Woolard, John	979	Younghusband, R.	1136
Whiting, William	769				

Grantees Carleton,

1783.

Andrew, George	26	
Andrew, Robert	168	
Austin, Caleb	28	
Adams, James 159	170	
Adnett,	209	
Armstrong, Richard	233	
Ambrose, Michael	332	
Ambrose, Margaret	355	
Anderson, James	245	
Allen, John	363	
Brothers, Joseph	8	
Brothers, William	417	
Brickley, James	36	
Bowman, Andrew	41	
Beaty, Edward, jr.	70	
Beaty, Edward, sr.	71	
Beaty, Polly	72	
Beaty, Joseph	129	
Beaty, William	130	
Brawn, Richard	89	
Blair, David	109	
Britton, John	135	
Byles, Mather, jr.	137	
Bonel, Joseph	163	
Brundage, John	171	
Brundage, Jer. 256	257	
Bunce, Joseph 181	182	
Boyce, John (heirs)	204	
Barden, Peter	270	
Bean, John	407	
Burtis, William	286	
Blume, John L.	408	
Blackee, James	305	
Brook, Jesse	317	
Barchus, John	318	
Bliss, Jonathan	341	
Bull, Richard	376	
Bought, John	380	
Bullerworth, Moses	390	
Bucket, William	418	
Clarke, William	120	
Colden, Thos. 121	122	
Corey, Gideon	162	
Camp, Hiel	161	
Camp, Neil	303	

Cox, William	163	
Crowel, Thomas	24	
Crowel, Sarah	377	
Crowel, Jos. 378 395	396	
Chew, Joseph	193	
Cathran, Alexander	194	
Chipman, Ward	195	
Campbell, Richard	29	
Campbell, Collin 100	101	
Campbell, Walt. 124	606	
Campbell, Don'd 160	172	
Campbell, Chas.	173	
Campbell, Hugh	444	
Campbell, Doug'd 604	605	
Cooper, Joseph	202	
Cooper, Edward	438	
Coffin, Wm. 30	285	
Coffin, John 223 224	242	
Coffin, John 243	602	
Coffin, Jonathan	241	
Coffin, Isaac	244	
Coffin, Thomas A.	281	
Coffin, Nathaniel	246	
283 384 385 386	603	
Cock, John, jr.	205	
Cock, John, sr.	206	
Cock, Sarah	212	
Cock, William	437	
Cock, Kelah	507	
Clayton	210	
Carpenter, Wm. 347	309	
Cougle, Jno. 249 611	612	
Craft, John	296	
Cully, John	298	
Cozens, Samuel	416	
Drummond, Jacobina	81	
Drummond, Ann	82	
Drummond, Alex.	105	
Drummond, Ann	106	
Davis, Burrow 111	112	
Duffell, James	127	
Duffell, Edward	320	
Dowling, Lawrence	153	
Dominick, Francis	169	
Dowling, Abraham	216	

Davison, J.	239 424 425	
Dickenson, Nat'l	428 436	
Dickenson, Hannah	548	
Ellis, Jesse	126	
Erskin, Chas.	132 133	
Esk, John L.	150	
Eccles, James	315	
Fennemore, Richard	55	
Fay, Henry E.	92 93 94	
	95 138 139	
Frink, Nathan	110 123	
	250 251	
Forester, Mary	131	
Freeman, Lewis	190	
Frazer, William	337	
Frazer, Lewis	380	
Frazer, Oliver	351	
Frazer, James	426 427	
Faulkner, John	441	
Forbes, James	44	
Gilles, Archibald 1	613	
Gerean, Barnett	22	
Gerrard, William	69	
Glazier, Bearmsly (heirs		
	156 157	
Glover, Andrew	213	
Hutchinson, Wm. 13	106	
Hutchinson, John	44	
Holland, John 113	114	
Holland, Richard	57	
Holland, Hannah	59	
Holland, Rich'd D.	68	
Holland, Joseph W.	134	
Halliblade, Peter	42	
Horn, Peter	74	
Hamilton, George	87	
Hoyt, Stephen	107	
Hoyt, Stephen J.	333	
Hoyt, Joseph Z.	334	
Harris George,	118	
Harris, William	125	
Hales, Harris W. 140	141	
Hill, John	174	
Henderson, John	200	
Howser, Jacob	208	

Name	No.	Name	No.	Name	No.
Wetmore, Luther	295	Wilson, Jacob	300 301	Weaver, Frederick	420
Wetmore, Thomas	311	Ward Jacob	313	Young, William	9
Wetmore, John	368	Ward, John	314	Young, Henry	33
Wetmore, William	367	Willard, Abijah	345	Young, Peter	34 80
Watson, John	278	Wood, Joseph	346	Young, Abraham	79
Williamson, Geo.	279	Welling, William	393	Years, Thomas	103
Wright, Thomas	283	Welling, Peter	394	Yeomans, Ely	327
Wright, Alexander	321	Weaver, George	419